'Imagine entering a new/old ci
Imagine seeking guidance to tha
streets, underground connections
eyed, multilingual, even minded. ʌ
the discernment of a wolf. This ʃ
Zurich. She sets the City within fluid ontologies of indigenous mentalities, the beginnings of things and the continuum. She re-minds that relatedness is the essence of human nature. Here is a guide who does not bow to the icons, yet takes you, with care, through the bewildering City. The maze of psychotherapy.'

Craig San Roque, *psychotherapist and author,*
Alice Springs, Australia

'*Therapy: The Basics* is an excellent resource for anyone interested in understanding more about approaches to therapy, their histories, similarities, and differences. The span of theories and their associated approaches is extensive and includes those that are not often included in volumes on psychotherapy such as body psychotherapy, eco therapy, psychodrama, and the arts therapies. However, Iykou goes even further than the usual Western methods, by including information on non-Western understandings of emotional health "traditional indigenous healing practices." Indigenous peoples from each continent are represented in this wonderfully informative chapter. Indeed, the chapter is the true gem of the book in my estimation. It contains valuable and fascinating information that hopefully fills a gap for both professionals and nonprofessionals alike. It is easy to imagine this book inspiring many readers to further exploration and greater understanding.'

Robyn Flaum Cruz, *professor, Lesley University*
Department of Expressive Therapies, USA

'For those who are beginning their training as therapists, *Therapy: The Basics* offers a first broad view to different theories in psychotherapy, in an accessible language. For those who have been trained in a single theoretical perspective, it is a valuable resource to expand their conceptual referents in their work. And for those of us who have purposefully explored and learned from different approaches, this book helps us to revisit already known perspectives and to integrate new ones to enrich our training, while encouraging us to keep dialoguing, from concrete practice, with several theoretical frameworks.

I value the author's recognition that the different proposals, as well as the practice of therapy, are delimited and conditioned by the sociocultural system, the epoch, and the countries where they have been developed and validated. The inclusion of a chapter on non-Western models of psychotherapy has been an invitation and a reminder of dialogues, readings and activities waiting to be done to advance in the understanding of the cosmologies and philosophies of life of so many human groups that live in a marginalised world or in conflict with the so-called Western culture.'

Salvador Moreno López, *psychotherapist and retired professor, Instituto Tecnológico y de Estudios Superiores in Guadalajara, México*

'In this thorough undertaking to chart the history of approaches to therapy globally, sissy expertly points out connections among diverse theorists. She weaves a narrative of how therapy has arisen from the colonial anthropocentric project but with the potential to catch all its socially, politically, and relationally aware threads. In so doing, there is the potential to disrupt the perpetuation of hierarchical systems of inequalities and to transform the wellbeing agenda into one focused on interdependence, harmony and local and grass roots knowledge. This book is a must read for all aspiring and current students of therapy and all practising therapists who want to broaden and challenge the situated nature of their chosen theoretical approach.'

Gillian Proctor, *PhD, lecturer in counselling and psychotherapy, University of Leeds, UK*

'Therapy can be a minefield to the uninitiated, and if you really want to understand it, you probably need a hand to guide you through all the complexity. The gentle hand offered by sissy lykou in this comprehensive yet accessible text guides the reader through everything they need to know including the history and development of different approaches, their theories, practices, and terminologies. Going far beyond "the usual suspects" lykou takes a thoroughly contemporary approach by contextualising the field in the light of a cross-cultural and intersectional lens, ensuring that the rich texture of our diverse field is represented in all its facets. A must read for anyone wishing to learn more about what therapy is today.'

Aaron Balick, *PhD, psychotherapist and author, UK*

'sissy lykou has written a hugely informative book not just for therapists but also for clients, mapping a thorough and accessible overview of therapeutic theories and practice, their points of divergence and convergence, and that importantly acknowledges the psy-disciplines' indebtedness to indigenous wisdom traditions.'

Rebecca Esho Greenslade, *(she/her), psychotherapist and founder, The Feminist Therapy Network*

THERAPY

Therapy: The Basics is an introductory book to psychotherapy and its different theoretical approaches. It attempts to demystify and de-stigmatise therapy by answering some common questions posed by prospective clients.

lykou presents an accessible overview of psychotherapy and counselling, mapping a variety of the most popular approaches from psychoanalysis and cognitive behaviour therapy to embodied and creative therapies, whilst giving an overview of the roots of psychotherapy in traditional and indigenous healing methods. The book also acknowledges criticisms of current approaches, with their neo-liberal heteronormative Eurocentric perspective, and considers where therapy stands in today's globalised world. The book's structure allows different umbrella theories and their developments to be explored separately but also in relation to one another.

This book is essential reading for trainees, a useful reference for qualified therapists who want to deepen their knowledge, a supporting resource for prospective psychotherapy clients, and a companion for readers who simply want to expand their horizons.

sissy lykou practises in London privately and in community therapy projects and is interested in the interplay between psychotherapy, the arts, and politics.

The Basics Series

The Basics is a highly successful series of accessible guidebooks which provide an overview of the fundamental principles of a subject area in a jargon-free and undaunting format.

Intended for students approaching a subject for the first time, the books both introduce the essentials of a subject and provide an ideal springboard for further study. With over 50 titles spanning subjects from artificial intelligence (AI) to women's studies, *The Basics* are an ideal starting point for students seeking to understand a subject area.

Each text comes with recommendations for further study and gradually introduces the complexities and nuances within a subject.

For a full list of titles in this series, please visit www.routledge.com/The-Basics/book-series/B

THERAPY
THE BASICS

sissy lykou

Routledge
Taylor & Francis Group

LONDON AND NEW YORK

Designed cover image: vaitekune © Getty Images

First published 2025
by Routledge
4 Park Square, Milton Park, Abingdon, Oxon OX14 4RN

and by Routledge
605 Third Avenue, New York, NY 10158

Routledge is an imprint of the Taylor & Francis Group, an informa business

ISBN: 978-0-367-42470-1 (hbk)
ISBN: 978-0-367-42472-5 (pbk)
ISBN: 978-0-367-82433-4 (ebk)

DOI: 10.4324/9780367824334

Typeset in Bembo
by Apex CoVantage, LLC

To Michalis, my first and eternal therapist

CONTENTS

AUTHOR BIOGRAPHY

sissy lykou is a UKCP-registered psychotherapist, embodied movement psychotherapist and supervisor. She practices in London privately and has been developing innovative therapeutic-educational projects for children under 5 and their parents/carers in several children's centres in London. She is now an independent academic and lectures on several university and professional training programmes in the UK and Europe, after a career in academia and leading psychotherapy training courses. sissy has also worked on EU research projects at the Universities of Heidelberg and Athens.

She has published in books and international journals and is the co-editor of the book *Trauma in the Creative and Embodied Therapies: When Words Are Not Enough* by Routledge. Her professional experience also includes being an editorial board member of international journals.

sissy is interested in the interplay between psychotherapy, the arts, and politics.

www.lykoucounselling.co.uk

ACKNOWLEDGEMENTS

This book has been a long and adventurous journey, travelled with the support of several beloved people in my life, and mostly written during the several lockdowns of the pandemic.

Thank you

- . . . Sarah Rae for your empathic guidance in submitting the final product.
- . . . Craig San Roque for your generous and knowledgeable support in finding information and inspiration to write about Australian Aboriginal healing practices.
- . . . Foluke Taylor for your warm nudge to connect deeper with my unruly writing intentions and for your generous feedback.
- . . . Professor Claire Schaub-Moore and Professor Nicolas Christakis for your belief in my work and constant encouragement that gave me wings to fly at the beginning of my career.
- . . . Spiros for all your kindness and generosity in offering to play the role of my personal librarian.
- . . . my courageous intellectual family for all your support and nurturing: Cat, Lynne, Ioanna, Jamie, Nicki, Niki, Rashida, and Roz.
- . . . Suzanne for your comradery and consistently accepting and caring presence in my life.

. . . Paul and Pieter, the unique Bistis, for being my rocks in all my creative ventures.

. . . Shane for taking me to magical places so that I feel inspired to write.

. . . mum, my sister Maria, and nephews, Yiorgos and Agelos for always providing the warmest hugs in the world.

. . . dad, for giving me the first vocabulary of resistance – I miss you deeply.

My biggest thanks go to all my clients and supervisees who have always had an impact on how I see, practise, and embody therapy – you are my best teachers!

INTRODUCTION

WHY THERAPY: MYTHS, FANTASIES, AND OTHER INTERESTING THOUGHTS ABOUT WHAT HAPPENS IN THE CONSULTING ROOM

I often get asked to describe what I do as a therapist, having to explain that there are more kinds of therapy than cognitive behaviour therapy (CBT) – the seemingly dominant approach in today's society – and having to de-stigmatise therapy as something that all of us can access at some point in our lives, if we want so. I also often find myself speaking about how inspired I am by recent shifts in the profession to a more integrated model of a mind-body continuum and focus, with an openness to creativity. The latter seems to be an ongoing theme as our society tends to idealise either our mind or our body and to allocate creativity to artists.

I have also been involved in therapy projects that aim to bring therapy outside the consulting room, so that people do not feel scared or intimidated by the prospect of having or studying therapy. This is important work – if people aren't able to easily access information on the different therapeutic approaches, how can they access therapy to help themselves and others? Often, I am asked to help friends and acquaintances to find a therapist given the plethora of approaches and the lack of clarity on who is doing what.

DOI: 10.4324/9780367824334-1

Similarly, if the different theoretical schools and employment prospects are not explained somehow, somewhere, isn't it a problem for prospective students who might not be totally sure about the choice of the approach they want to train in?

So, what better way to demystify therapy and its different approaches for the general public and future students than a book on the basics of therapy? By using the more generic terms *therapy* and *therapists*, I intend to bring together psychotherapy, counselling, the embodied and creative therapies, and traditional healing so that there is a unified (or at least clarified) image of the therapy map for the reader. You will notice that I refer to *clients* throughout the book apart from the chapter on psychoanalysis and the psychodynamic approaches. In the psychoanalytic tradition the terms that are used are *patient* – or sometimes *analysand* – and *analyst*, and I have used these terms in my writing too. Also, I prefer to use the pronouns they/them for therapists and clients as it feels the least gender-based way of describing the individuals involved.

The choice of more contemporary language (versus academic) has been intentional; I aim to explore theory, research, and practice in relation to therapy using accessible language so this book can be read by people of all backgrounds. I aim for my work to be part of the movement that tries to democratise academic information. Although I also wish that this is a book that can be used by all therapists whenever a need comes up for understanding each other's approach or updating their frame of knowledge in our field.

This book also aims to acknowledge the limitations caused by the neo-liberal heteronormative Eurocentricity of therapy trainings and practices and will approach the discipline from a critical perspective. The order of chapters, therefore, intends to disrupt the imposed Western narratives of what is therapy and to acknowledge the long, and ongoing, marginalisation of certain groups in our world.

What I will not try to do, though, is to give clinical cases as examples for each theory. You will be able to access some examples in the suggested readings at the end of each chapter and/or section. This is because, again, this is a book intended to be read by the wider public and therefore any clinical material could complicate the reader in their effort to imagine each theory.

How often have you caught yourself wondering what happens in your friend's/partner's/child's/parent's therapy?

What is your fantasy of a first therapy session?

Do you feel that your images of therapy are mainly influenced by movies and TV series and if yes, what comes first to mind?

How did you choose your first therapist?

What were the influences in your choice of your therapy training?

WHEN AND WHERE IT ALL BEGAN: A HISTORICAL JOURNEY FROM THE 19TH-CENTURY CASES OF HYSTERIA TO TODAY'S ONLINE AND HYBRID THERAPY

It is hard to define when it all began. We could even perceive the ancient Greek theatre plays as therapy, given their aim for *catharsis*; or the Australian aboriginal storytelling with their aim of connecting with the self and nature. Traditional indigenous healing practices (see Chapter 1) are definitely the roots of therapy as a practice that resembles what we now know in the Western world, and then maybe we can trace back some of the fundamentals of more theorised therapy work in the late 19th century and the work of Wilhelm Wundt, the father of experimental psychology. We can see in his work the first attempt for the epistemological stance that Western psychology and psychotherapy have always strived for, as well as the first glimpses of understanding the development of personality. At around the same time Ambroise-Auguste Liébeault and Hippolyte Bernheim at the Nancy School (Suggestion School) postulated that hypnotism with suggestions brings change and that the effects of hypnotism can equally be reached through suggestions to a woken patient; they called this *psychotherapeutics*. Jean-Martin Charcot and the Paris School (Salpêtrière School) was the centre of hypnosis, and it was Charcot who mentioned the existence of unconscious ideas as the origin of neuroses and made connections between psycho-physical symptoms and psychic trauma. Pierre Janet, Charcot's protégé, tried to answer the question of 'how' through analysis and synthesis. His work was also based on the ideas of dissociation of memories and the loss of connection with the reality; two principles which, alongside his coined term of the *subconscious*, very clearly influenced Sigmund Freud (see Chapter 2). Eugen Bleuler at the Burghölzli coined the terms *schizophrenia* and *ambivalence* and, influenced by Freud, encouraged his team to work with patients based on the idea of the unconscious. Jung's 'word association test' was developed during his time with Bleuler at the Burghölzli. Josef Breuer is best known as Freud's mentor at the latter's first steps in understanding and using hypnosis for the treatment of hysteria. Before then, though, Breuer had made a breakthrough with his case of Anna O. and his *cathartic method* which was a form of hypnosis for processing trauma. There is no doubt, though, that it was Freud's ideas that sent a ripple of shock waves to the widely held beliefs of the then society, and we could even compare their impact to that caused by Copernicus's finding about the Earth as one, and not the only, planet. After the *Studies of Hysteria*, which he co-wrote with Breuer, Freud started his solo writing journey and his 1900 *The Interpretation of Dreams* would change the Western world forever. Since then there has been a flourishing and diverse attempt to define the structure of personality and psychopathology, resulting in the theories of personality and therapy that we will be exploring in the next few chapters. But what is a theory of personality?

A theory of personality is a framework that gives a description of the person, of what goes on for them and how their behavioural and emotional material can be organised, as well as an explanation of the phenomena (i.e. issues, processes, dysfunctions, etc.) under study. All theories of personality try to make meaning of being human in the world, to explain the essential relationships between the person and the world, and to account for human experiences and human behaviour. Looking at theories of personality in this way we can understand why they also include predictions of future events for subsequent evaluation, and a potential set of practical applications – in the form of 'how to' in therapy and in other fields, such as family or education – for control of processes, dynamics, and symptoms.

The profound discoveries made by the theorists we will explore in the next few chapters are based on clinical observations. The theorists' own lives are mostly their empirical materials; thus, their theories and hypotheses regarding human nature are coloured by their subjective experiential worlds and their personal perception of existence as an individual. All theories are also dependent on their social and historical environment, and you might want to look up what was happening in the world when each of the following theorists developed their theory and practice.

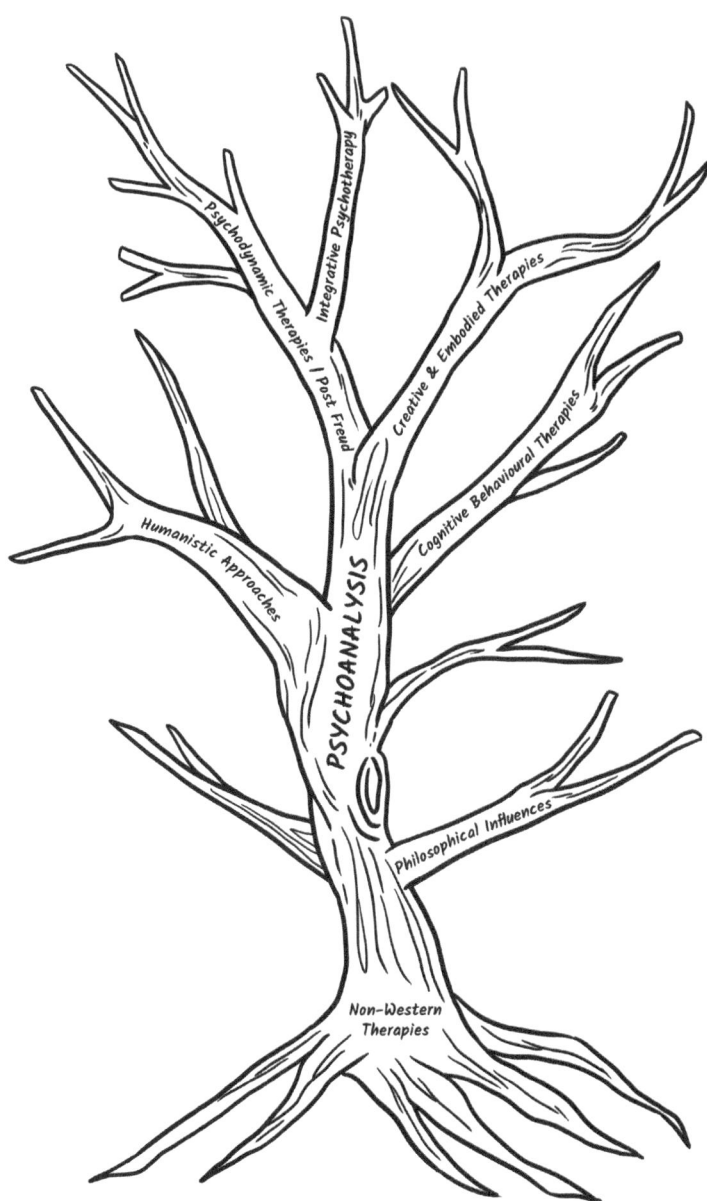

The tree of therapy – designed by Joe Winfield

The end of the Second World War found the therapy field – and the world – in desperate need for a more equal society and for better understanding of human nature. Therapy needed to be more accessible, with more democratic terms, and there was a generalised need to know one's self and to answer the question 'What makes us fully and optimally human?' Humanistic therapies started developing then but mainly flourished in the 1960s and 1970s with the libertarian ethos of those decades placing the main focus of therapy on the concept of self-actualisation.

At the same time humanistic therapies were called the third force because they entered the long-term competition between behavioural-cognitive therapies that were established in the 1950s and 1960s, and psychodynamic therapies with all their long history and authority.

Whilst all these more political fights for establishment of the 'strongest' approach were taking place, new approaches under these three umbrellas developed with the expressive and embodied therapies taking different forms and shapes according to each continent's focus, and with the more recent developments of outdoor therapy, online therapy, and hybrid (a combination of online and in-person) forms of therapy listening to the needs of the modern human.

Consequently, the image of therapy has been changing according to which part of the tree we are looking at, and which decade. A very first image of therapy is at the roots of the tree with all the traditional and indigenous healing practices practised in connection to nature and communities. Then classical psychoanalysis becomes the trunk of the tree projecting an image of therapy with the patient lying on the couch and the analyst sitting behind them and keeping notes. As we move upwards on the tree trunk, we cannot but include the philosophical influences on all Western theories. Even further up on the branches, the image of therapy gradually changes to two people sitting on chairs and opposite each other. And the image changes again when we look at the flexibility required in the creative arts therapies and in the outdoor-based therapies, where therapist and client are in a constant negotiation of positioning themselves in the therapy space.

Therapists in today's world work in many and diverse settings: hospitals, prisons, care homes, schools, businesses, rehabilitation centres, even in war zones. Training takes a few years and it depends on the approach and the country, with each country having one or more professional bodies overseeing the trainings and practice of its members. Therapists also work as researchers and it is important to highlight here the development on qualitative and quantitative research in the field since the '50s – although Freud's case studies are also a form of qualitative research.

This book is structured in such a way that the different 'umbrella theories' and their developments can be explored separately but also in relation to each other. For all those 'umbrella theories' I have chosen to focus on as many of their developments as possible, but I acknowledge that the list is not exhaustive and that the reader will need to look up more specific sources. At the end of each chapter or section you will find: (1) some recommended reading that I feel will help you find more information in an accessible way, and (2) a more detailed and extensive list of references I used.

So, sit back and try to be and remain open-minded about the different theories, to engage your whole mind-body in your reading, and to adopt a different outlook in each chapter and section. The floating tables with reflective questions might help you in getting into this body-mind space.

RECOMMENDED READING

Freedheim, D. (2002). *History of psychotherapy: A century of change.* Washington, DC: American Psychological Association.
Walter, M., & Fridman, E. (Eds.). (2004). *Shamanism: An encyclopedia of world beliefs, practices and culture.* Santa Barbara, CA: ABC-CLIO.

REFERENCES

Dryden, W., & Reeves, A. (2012). *The handbook of individual therapy* (6th ed.). London: Sage.
Ewen, R. B. (2010). *An introduction to theories of personality* (7th ed.). New York: Psychology Press.
Haugh, S., & Paul, S. (Eds.). (2008). *The therapeutic relationship: Perspectives and themes.* Ross-on-Wye: PCCS Books.

NON-WESTERN MODELS OF PSYCHOTHERAPY
UNDERSTANDING EMOTIONAL WELL-BEING IN INDIGENOUS TRADITIONAL HEALING WAYS

This chapter will focus on indigenous traditional healing from all over the world, as opposed to the limited idea that when we talk about psychotherapy, we mean only the Western theories and practices explored in the following chapters. We can define Western therapies as colonial and post-colonial Anglo–Saxon approaches that responded to their medicalised world, whilst non-Western therapies include the pre-Christianity healing practices that didn't pathologise human phenomena. There is a difference between therapy as healing and as treatment.

I will try to create some context about why it is vital to include traditional healing in this generic therapy book, especially considering the mental health crisis our world is going through after the pandemic.

Let's start by thinking about the concepts of *universality* and *universalism*, two clearly Western concepts. The first is about one theory explaining and providing understanding about everything. The second is about one theory being applicable everywhere. A prominent example of these two concepts is the use of diagnostic manuals (e.g. diagnostic and statistical manual of mental disorders (DSM) and the international classification of diseases (ICD)) for the diagnosis of mental health problems, and the consequent use of governmental guidelines to decide what is the best therapy approach for each

DOI: 10.4324/9780367824334-2

diagnosis. This phenomenon, though, of 'one for everything' is based on essentialism (i.e. unchanged universal qualities) and neutrality of theory across cultures. In other words, mental/emotional health is seen from one prism across cultures and therefore certain theories and practices are accepted and promoted.

It is, therefore, obvious that we are talking about the impact of colonialism on mental health views and services. The domination of the Western medical model has been imposed on non-Western cultures – and societies – and has consequently underestimated and erased indigenous knowledge, wisdom, and practices. The medical model, as it stands now, derives from what is learnt and applied in the metropolitan hubs of 'developed' countries (usually the Northern hemisphere) and disregards the impact of geopolitical and geopsychological factors, which means that the experience of the global majority is erased. Medicalisation has also taken humans away from the ecosystemic, contextual, and political perspectives – vital components of indigenous healing – on distress and healing. Indigenous health systems broadly start from a place of individual and group connection with the health of our ecosystem. The threats of deforestation, mining, and climate crisis in addition to the Westernisation of mental health practices pose yet another danger for the extinction of traditional healing practices.

To see the extent of the effects of colonialism in 'othering' non-Western cultures even in theories and services for mental health, it might be helpful to consider the results from a 2015 *Lancet Psychiatry* review. The authors reported a 20–80% range of patients' use of traditional and other complementary forms of medicine for mental health problems. They then highlighted the difficulties in defining and classifying traditional healing practices and means and, I would like to add, the inherent difficulty of scattered information due to centuries of colonial oppression that led many traditional healers and their communities to hide their practices.

This chapter is an homage to all those practices, rituals, and traditions that persevered as cultural therapies and managed to survive the global colonisation of certain European nations and their ongoing legacy of subjugation and dispossession. It is a testament of their use and effectiveness about which numerous articles, reviews, and books have been written – either by indigenous or by white people. After all, the West have exoticised shamans since the '60s and from daemonic charlatans (see during Enlightenment); they are now finally seen and recognised for their psychotherapeutic efficacy through their healing rituals and practices. As I write this, I can't stop but thinking that the position I am in (i.e. a white therapist living and working in Europe) runs the risk of 'othering' when I write about 'other' cultures, and I invite you also to consider your position and subsequent actions when you read this chapter.

To conclude my reasoning about this chapter I will quote the psychoanalysts Jean Laplanche and Jean-Bertrand Pontalis who defined psychotherapy as '[i]n a broad sense – any method of treating psychic or somatic disorders which utilises psychological means or more specifically – the therapist–patient relationship . . . [including] hypnosis, suggestion, psychological re-education, persuasion, etc'. (1973: 373). Which then means that any traditional healing practices based on the use of psychological means and the therapist–patient relationship fits into the category of psychotherapy as the West defines this. The difference, though, might be that any traditional healing practice is perceived and received neither as invasive nor as imperialistic; it can be an empowering input on an individual, family, social, and spiritual level. And this is what some countries have achieved (see later e.g. Australia or Ecuador) by developing structures where the traditional healthcare systems co-exist with the official healthcare systems, an achievement of integration that has come as a result of the conscious efforts to support continuity between traditional healers and the formal health system.

Definition of traditional healing and traditional medicine

Traditional medicine is defined by the World Health Organization as

> the sum total of the knowledge, skills and practices based on theories, beliefs, and experiences indigenous to different cultures [. . .] used in the maintenance of health, as well as in the prevention, diagnosis, improvement or treatment of physical and mental illnesses.

These include rituals, forms of talking and counselling, supernatural remedies, religious scripts, herbs, etc.

It is beyond the capacity of this book to include all traditional healing practices, so I will concentrate on the verbal and non-verbal practices (e.g. rituals, dances, and storytelling) and will not be including

Chinese medicine, Ayurveda, Ayahuasca, or any other plant hallucinogen drugs and herbs. I refer the reader to sources specific to those practices. I am also providing a landscape of the practices and approaches towards mental health rather than the whole functioning range of traditional healers as they deal with various ailments.

I will use a categorising system of practices by continent as I feel it will help you, the reader, to visualise the landscapes, people, and the other than human involved in each healing tradition, and I will give some examples from each continent. The choice of examples was practical in the sense of how much information was possible to be accessed online (i.e. journal articles, websites, and books) and/or via discussions with therapy colleagues in all continents.

But before we go there let's see some basic shared concepts and principles amongst the many and diverse practices of traditional healing:

- The issues people experience, and for which they reach out to traditional healers, are seen as interrelated with history, life experiences, and the sociopolitical context, rather than something that exists within themselves. The suffering individual can be the voice of what is suffering in the family/community. The group, family, and the community are, therefore, seen as connected to the issues and quite often participate in the rituals and healing process.
- Well-being as a concept and as an emotional state depends on the social, emotional, cultural, and spiritual aspects of an individual's health, and all these layers need to be addressed during the healing process. Traditional healing addresses the body–mind–spirit connection.
- Any issues that have to do with an individual's emotional and mental health are categorised through either a symptom-focused method or a cause-focused one (see here the similarities with the Western biomedical model).
- Traditional healers' practice is characterised by extensive listening of the healing-seekers' health complaints and their narration of their symptoms which is a crucial aspect for the building of trust and the aim for recovery. Traditional healers spend a long time with their clients, showing their empathy and engaging their clients as partners in the process (see similarities with Western psychotherapy).

- Traditional healers provide culturally appropriate explanations for any symptoms and suffering. Symptom meaning-making in an important part of the healing process and culturally sensitive care is connected to the aim for emotional well-being.
- Traditional healers are accessible (both travel-wise and financially) and provide a comfortable and familiar frame for healing. Trust in them is already established through their deep involvement and presence in their communities.

CONTINENT BY CONTINENT

AFRICA

South Africa

According to the South African department of health, by 2005 almost 70% of the population were consulting traditional healers. Traditional healers in South Africa are not a homogenous group, and there are certain categories of healers who have defined orientations but who also integrate elements from other orientations:

- Diviners: the name for a diviner varies from area to area. An *igqira* or *amagqira* or *sangoma* (*izangoma* in plural) has been given the power, through their ancestors, to divine the cause of illness. This power makes itself visible through *(uk)thwasa*; a South African culture-specific syndrome with a wide range of both physical and psychological symptoms that resemble the Western notion of a psychotic episode. *Izangoma* are responsible for their community's well-being and overall health but also for issues of justice that they see as connective and relational. They use bone-tossing, dream interpretation, and rituals for healing; they identify a mental health problem by the individual's behaviours; and they offer diverse diagnostic, divination, and counselling services that address emotional problems and distress.
- Herbalists: an *inyanga* or *igelda* or *bapedi* has the role of the Western pharmacist, but they dispense herbal remedies.
- Faith healers: a *mporofiti* or *umthandazi* works from within the African syncretic churches and their main treatment tools are prayers, singing, and holy water.

The Zulu South African notion of health is holistic and the product of a complex interaction between the individual, the spiritual, and the social contexts. Health is seen as a fine balance amongst the elements of the mind, the body, social factors, ancestral spirits, and the universe. Poor health is perceived as the consequence of bewitchment or possession or ancestral intervention, or because of natural causes. *Ubuntu* is the term that describes this collectivist emphasis on interdependency and harmony.

Despite the distinctive 'two-culture' reality for black people in South Africa, and the ongoing oppression of the colonial psychologising, there have been some important steps of legitimising traditional healers and their offer to their communities and the country. There is the Traditional Healers Organisation (THO) and the 2005/2007 Traditional Health Practitioners Act that aimed to recognise the cultural diversity in the health services; albeit the latter seems to have not been implemented yet.

Tanzania and Zanzibar

Traditional healers in modern Tanzania are called *fundi* (engineers/technicians). The original terms were *waganga wa kienyeji* or *waganga wa jadi*. Traditional healing rituals have a community target; they are there for the maintenance and restoration of everyone's well-being. The focus of treatment and prevention of symptoms and problems is on the quality of human relationships and social interactions.

There are four categories of traditional healers: (1) the diviners with diagnostic, healing, and spiritual roles; (2) the herbalists; (3) the herbalists-ritualists who combine herbal medicines and rituals for diagnosis and treatment; and (4) the faith healers using either the Qur'an or the Bible for healing purposes.

The connection to the spirits through rituals is for the purposes of both identifying the type and cause of illness, as well as for healing those spirits that are seen as responsible for the individual's problems.

Traditional healers in Tanzania are connected and acknowledged via their association Chama cha Waganga na Wakunga wa Tiba Asilia Tanzania (CHAWATIATA) that was founded in 1995.

Zanzibar as a semi-autonomous island and region of Tanzania have some similarities with the categorising of traditional healers (see herbalists, faith healers, diviners) but also a unique approach to collaboration between mainstream practitioners and traditional healers since 2008. The 'Zanzibar Traditional and Alternative Medicine Policy' recognises the potential of a closer relationship between formal and informal mental health practice.

ASIA

Bangladesh

In Bangladesh traditional healing practices are divided between religious (Kalami, Bhandari, and spiritual healing) and non-religious ones (sorcery, Kabiraji – medicinal plants and herbs – and home medicine). I will focus on the first category as the second one refers to mainly physical ailments or, in the case of sorcery, to imposing some sort of revenge on people. For religious healers the disorders they can cure are beyond natural phenomena and invisible – that is spiritual or mental. Traditional healing practices are also holistic, aiming to bring together the body, self, and society in a dynamic equilibrium.

Kalami is a healing system based on the verses of the Kalam (Qur'an), and it deals with spiritual difficulties that are clearly distinguished from physical illnesses. The Hujurs (Kalami healers) offer to cure a wide range of non-physical problems: from abolishing black magic to resolving family disputes – both causing emotional disturbance to an individual. Through the *bodna pora* diagnostic system, which involves a piece of paper with verses of the Kalam, the Hujur clarifies whether the problem is one they can deal with or whether they need to refer the person involved to the medical services. Treatments vary but drinking *pani pora* (invoked water) seems to be a usual one.

The Bhandari healing system offers to help people get rid of various difficulties, and it's based on Muslim faith too. The Bhandari healers are believed to have superpowers, and they use meditation and the connection with the ancestral spirit of Baba to diagnose the problem.

Spiritual healing in Bangladesh is mainly practised by Hindu women called Boiddya. Healing happens through the meditative practice of the Boiddya that allows them to communicate with diverse sacred spirits and pious ancestors. Treatments tend to be torturous, though, along with incantations, as the aim is to drive away all evil spirits. Spiritual healers often treat individuals who are discharged by medical facilities with failed treatment of their complex disease. Unquestionable faith is essential for anyone seeking the help of spiritual healers.

It seems that in Bangladesh people seek cures from religious healers without considering the religious perspective of the healers; thus, a Hindu can go to a Hujur and vice versa.

India

In a major country such as India, where the majority of the population live in rural areas, it is reported that traditional healers are the first stop for the care of mental health, given that the official psychological services provided by the national health system are based in town and cities. Traditional healers are easily accessible due to their local availability, and they can also provide culturally sensitive care.

Depending on the extent of the use of culture and religious causes for the emotional distress, and the chosen treatment method, healers are split between traditional ones and faith ones. The first are characterised by diversity in their view on emotional distress and their treatment methods:

- *Vaids:* practitioners of Ayurveda, the indigenous system of medicine that uses herbs and diet as a form of diagnosis and treatment.
- *Mantarwadis* and *Patris*: apart from healers, they also hold a role of problem-solving for business, farming, etc. Illness for both these categories of healers is caused by past transgressions, committed either by the suffering person or by their family – either in the present or previous lives. The Mantarwardis believe in the punitive power of Shiva, the God of destruction, and the treatment is based on rituals in certain Bhuta shrines that are connected to the suffering spirit. The Patris, on the other hand, are seen as the mediators between spirits, and their treatment offers a dialogue between their own master spirit (or demon) and the one of the suffering people. In this way, there is a means of accessing the suffering person's demon's wishes and acting accordingly.

Mental illness in India is perceived to have two factors: the causal ones (e.g. family problems), which also include addictions, and the spiritual ones. Somatisation, though, is not seen as mental illness, and it is believed to be the result of bewitchment when someone does well and certain people around them are jealous.

Japan

Japan's shamanic tradition can now be traced only in Okinawa, the group of islands to the south of mainland Japan. The traditional healers there are known by a number of terms: *yuta* (main island of Okinawa and Amami islands), *kankakarya/kaminohito* (Miyako district), and *munushiri* (used widely in Okinawa). All these terms basically mean a person possessed by the divine, a person of god and a knowledgeable person.

Yuta (using the most known term of all) is the traditional healer that projects life's problems on the malice of ancestors or the gods and facilitates rituals to tackle these. Yuta are mainly women, and they have gone through many different phases of suppression and persecution since the 17th century, especially during Japan's interest in Westernising its systems. But in Okinawa shamanism seems to be part of mainstream life and is perceived as the journey back to the base of the culture. Yuta have now come to play the role of therapists, functioning for the fulfilment of people's everyday needs and lives.

The initiator illness for seeing a yuta is called *kandaari/kamiburi*. This is a disorder with a set of symptoms that affect the individual's nervous system (e.g. audiovisual hallucinations), physical health (e.g. lack of appetite, body shaking), and everyday functioning (e.g. somnambulism, inability to perform daily duties).

For the Okinawa people illness is a familial, public, or multigenerational issue and can be managed through cooperative rituals. Treatment is seen within a bio-cultural context and spiritual possession is accepted, rather than seen as negative and therefore in need of elimination.

AUSTRALIA/OCEANIA

Australia

Despite the country's deeply ambivalent attitude to acknowledging the atrocities of the colonial people, there is a strong and committed movement for re-acculturation by Aboriginal people and white mental health workers. This is a movement that aims for recovery and healing as these are informed by, and rooted in, traditional Aboriginal medicine and law. The several projects I will refer to next have all been based on the principle of reconnecting with Aboriginal spirituality as the main means of healing.

In Aboriginal tradition the *Ngangakari* (or *Maparn*) is the traditional healer who can take any sickness away from people's bodies, thus giving them a sense of balance via removal. It is a process of equilibrium through re-finding some escaped spirits or chasing away some other spirits. It is a journey to reconnect with the practice of *Kanyini* that allows one to live in harmony and unconditional love. The spirit in Aboriginal tradition is essential in the breath and for a person to remain healthy, the spirit needs to be in its proper place.

Kurunpa is a concept congruent to the Western concept of the psyche or the soul. It is believed to be seated within the solar plexus and has the capacity/potential to be displaced, lost, injured, anxious or depressed, dissociated, or blocked in its function.

The Ngangakari project was initiated by the Ngaanyatjarra Pitjantjatjara Yankunytjatjara (NPY) Women's Council in the late '90s, and it brought traditional healing practices to the health system in Central Australia, after the mental health crisis among Aboriginal people reached a dead end and no conventional Western treatments seemed to be working. Improvement in the mental health of Aboriginal people was marked by the co-existence of Ngangakari and medical professionals in hospitals.

A further development of that project has been the Uti Kulintjaku (Clear Thinking) project since 2012. This is based on the Pitjantjatjara (Central Australian Aboriginal people and their language) understanding that to listen properly and understand are synonymous. This most recent project has been transferred beyond its original base in Central Australia, and it provides a bridge between the psychological and the behavioural forces (e.g. in the case of alcohol addiction). Words for various states of minds are the focus here. Skilled interpreters facilitate the process so that people can think in their own language, express themselves in depth and with all the subtlety that psychological work requires. The project is now well established, and the process and results have been disseminated via books, an app, magnets with emotional language in Pitjantjatjara and English, and a poster that depicts in images and in bilingual language various emotional and mental states.

These projects have been successful due to some long-trusted cross-cultural relationships, the active engagement of Aboriginal people and their wishes and needs, equality in and respect for different kinds of knowledge and different ways of being, as well as continuous processing of what is there and what changes.

This two-way vision and understanding has created the *potential space*, in Winnicott's words, for work in this area of two worlds. White people in this process of developing a balanced and fair intercultural attitude also have the ethical responsibility to deconstruct their Western views and expectations and develop an indigenous-informed awareness of the indigenous people's reality and context, whilst also having direct relationship with the communities on the ground.

Another long-term and well-established psychological project in Australia is the 'Marumali Journey of Healing' and the 'Marumali Programme'. This is a programme that was conceived and developed by Lorraine Peeters, an Aboriginal and Torres Strait islander survivor of the governmental forcible removal from their families and institutionalisation of children from these communities. Peeters went through a self-journey for five years in the mid '90s and from that journey she developed the Marumali Programme that is now facilitated and taught throughout the whole country. She describes her project as a healing one rather than a therapy/treatment one, as she sees the survivors of the removal policies and the 'Stolen Generation' as a social and emotional issue, and not a mental health issue.

Marumali is the word for healing ('put back together') in Kamilaroi, and the journey is one of recovery, with the holistic engagement of mind–body–spirit–culture–identity and the reconnection with one's family, community, and country.

Aotearoa New Zealand

Aotearoa New Zealand first banned all indigenous healing practices in 1907 with the Tohunga Suppression Act (TSA). Any Māori soul healing or intervention was eliminated, and the psychotherapeutic community is reported to have taken an apolitical stance over the years.

Since the mid '70s though, some contemporary Māori views have been developed (e.g. *Te Whare Tapa Wha or Te Pae Mahutonga*) that emphasise the centrality of the family (*Whānau*) and the interconnectedness of the spiritual (*taha wairua*)-the physical (*taha tinana*)-the mind (*taha hinengaro*), for the achievement of health and well-being.

In the Māori tradition the *tohunga makutu* is the shaman who holds a wide range of healing repertoire that involves physical treatments, the use of touch, working with symbols and dreams, infusions, and water therapy. Their approach is one that tries to understand human and other than human interactions, within a certain cultural context, and to find the problem within any relationship breakdown. Tohunga also have the role of the intermediary between the individual in suffering and their families, community, and society. For the Māori culture there is no division between physical and emotional illness, and this is represented in both experience and language. *Pukiri* (fury/hostility) and *manawa-pouri* (sadness) are two distinctive examples; the first is a feeling located in the stomach (*puku*), whilst the latter links anxiety and depression with the heart (*manawa*) rather than the mind.

The first intercultural mental health service in Aotearoa New Zealand was at Tokanui psychiatric hospital in 1981, where some Māori mental health professionals set up the Whai Ora unit, a Māori cultural unit with a certain framework to guide psychiatric nursing. This is a model that managed to incorporate *taha wairua, taha whanau, taha hinengaro, taha tinana, taha whenua* (environment), *taha tikanga* (compliance), *Māoritanga* (old world), *Pakehatanga* (new world), and *taha tangata* (self). Te reo Māori was spoken and the day was structured according to Māori protocols. This way of operating created a shared sense of pride between service users and staff about their cultural identity and increased cultural knowledge and skill. Western methods and treatments were also incorporated.

The Ngā Ao e Rua project is another example of psychotherapy inter-cultural work that started in 2004 and involves indigenous and non-indigenous therapists and healthcare providers who have been trying to bridge the gap in the field, created by the monocultural attitude of Western psychotherapy. It is an ongoing experiment in biculturalism.

The Waka Oranga project is a further development that has been putting into practice the acculturation of psychotherapy. In this project Māori and Pākehā (white/European descent)/Tauiwi (all people on non-Māori descent) apply the contemporary Māori health perspectives that highlight the necessity for culturally relevant translations of health, a wider understanding of health, and a balance between the Western medical model and the respect of social and cultural factors. The group of health providers engaged in this project are advocates of the importance of acculturation in the theory and practice of psychotherapy so that both Māori clients' and practitioners' needs can be met. For this to happen, professional and community consciousness is developed, and the core relational and traditional Māori concepts are used to promote healing. Intra-psychic processes are also placed into the context in which one lives – including processes such as environmental guardianship and sustainability, social justice, and spiritual fulfilment. For the Waka Oranga practitioners, a Māori psychotherapy needs to be relational, contextual, spiritual, and inclusive.

EUROPE

Ireland

I have chosen to include Ireland in this chapter as Irish people and culture lost their indigenous healing practices as colonised people with white skin. Before the British colonisation that imposed Christianity, Ireland held a holistic healing shamanic model that was deeply rooted in the spiritual energy of the land and nature's cycles. The focus of healing was on natural soulful empowerment with the retrieval of souls requiring the calling of spirits, good and bad ones. The shamanic tradition was passed on to the generations orally, and mythology, archetypes, and sacred sites held the tradition.

The three classes of holy people were the *seers* (future tellers), the *bards* (song and story-tellers), and the *druids*. The latter fulfilled the healing roles as they were able to converse with supernatural powers and exist in an 'in-between' state, giving them a liminal nature. Within the druid class there were also the more experienced healers, the ovates, who held a vast and unique knowledge of the healing properties of plants.

In Irish indigenous healing, people's emotional ups and downs were associated with the activities of the Otherworld beings. The druid then had to restore the balance with the fairy world. The known healing practices are: sacrifices, chanting, using the druidic breath (*anál druidecht*), herbs and water (healing well rituals), laying on sticks of rowan, and looking at clouds (*néladoracht*)-listening to the bird voices-calling/summoning the spirits (*toghairm*).

Irish traditional healing grew out of a magico-religious belief system, so tales and poetry were equally important to the natural elements and the wisdom of the Otherworld.

NORTH AMERICA (INCLUDING THE COUNTRIES THAT MAKE UP CENTRAL AMERICA AND THE CARIBBEAN/WEST INDIES)

Greenland

Greenland is situated between the Arctic and Atlantic oceans but belongs to the Kingdom of Denmark (see European colonies). Although there is no surviving traditional healing practice of the indigenous Inuit culture after the Christian missionaries of the early 18th century, several neo-shamanic movements in the West have revived what seems to have been the *angakok's* (Inuit shaman) work. Inuits believed in all humans having a name, body, and soul, with the two latter being connected but with the potential to separate. So, illness was seen as the loss of soul from the body but also as the possession of other souls or spirits (from animals or human) by the body. Psychological problems were a body and soul illness. Angakoks could be women or men, and they saw their work not as a profession but as an ability. Their main healing principles were soul retrieval, battle with evil spirits, and protection against evil spirits, and the means of healing were shamanic journeying by *inngerutit* (drum singing), *serratit* (incantations), and *arnussat* (amulets). The first could be seen to serve a variety of purposes related to emotional venting, social positioning, and entertainment.

Today's Greenland involves a movement towards more culturally sensitive therapy approaches, as well as towards the introduction of healing practices from the pre-colonial Inuit culture (e.g. young people's therapy services being offered in nature as this is seen as part of the Inuit's belief that people and environment are parts of the same wholeness).

Guatemala

A holistic indigenous healthcare practice in Guatemala consists of the Mayan healers '*curandero*' (herbalist and folk healer) and '*guia*' (shaman – more of a spiritual guide).

In the Mayan system healers are granted the gift to heal, and it is not something one chooses or a career. Mind and body are interconnected; therefore, Mayan traditional healing is composed of the mind, body, religion, ritual, and science systems.

The 'wellness seeker' is today's patient/client, and they are required to be active in the process of regaining their well-being (*raxnaq'il nuk'aslemal*). Alongside them there is the healer, their family, community members, the spiritual and natural realms, and they all create the therapeutic unit.

This is a practice that requires belief in the healer's ability to heal but equally, also, the wellness seeker's power to change.

Puerto Rico

An unincorporated territory of the USA, Puerto Rico's culture and traditions resemble much more its Caribbean and South American neighbours, and its traditional healing system is influenced by both its European and African ancestors.

Santeria and *espiritismo* have been the two traditional healing approaches and their main difference is in the way the healers – *santeros* and *espiritistas* – connect with the spirits for the diagnosis and treatment of an individual's problems.

Espiritismo, a religious as well as philosophical healing system, is based on the work of Leon H. Rivail, aka A. Kardec, a French spiritist in the 19th century. The main idea is that there is an invisible world populated by spirits which can penetrate the visible world and attach themselves to humans. The spirits can be incarnated as human beings or non-incarnated and thus disembodied, and they are arranged in a pyramid that starts with 'criminal' spirits and reaches the peak with the all-good universal spirit. Life is seen as a test of the spirits: if passed, then it can ascend the celestial hierarchy, whilst if failed, there is a demotion in rank and potential testing in the next incarnation.

Santeria has borrowed elements from the Yoruban (West African) traditions to combine them with its belief in the 15 saints. The core of this traditional healing approach is that there are some certain highly elevated spirits who have never been incarnated.

Both spiritist approaches, as a healing movement, found some recognition and legitimisation in the 19th century, and in the late 1970s, community mental health centres in Puerto Rico started an experiment, trying to integrate espiritismo within the public health system.

United States of America (USA) and Canada

Native American traditional healing practices in the USA and Canada faced centuries of suppression and near-extermination by the colonial authorities. Their rituals and practices persevered as cultural therapies and resisted the organised conquest, impoverishment, forced assimilation, and dispossession. All shared knowledge that supported positive health came under attack with the assimilation policies (see e.g. Residential School system) and was forced underground.

No wonder then that in Canada there is very little literature on indigenous approaches to healing, as well as little documentation or discussion on indigenous practices. There is also a lack of both Canadian and US indigenous health policy framework and a very narrow application and endorsement of indigenous well-being approaches, and these are usually led by community based or charity organisations.

Some well-established healthcare projects in the USA and Canada that provide culturally responsive care are as follows:

- Anishnawbe Health Toronto, an accredited community health centre that works with traditional healers, elders, medicine people, and Western healthcare professionals in a holistic approach to overcoming barriers to health and improvement of life standards. Trauma, abuse, addiction, homelessness, and poverty are part of the aims of this project that overall has a core focus on connecting to identity and culture as a means to healthy paths. Traditional healing, traditional medicines, and participation in ceremonies are offered to all service users by the Osh-ka-be-Wis (traditional helpers).
- The Dr. Agnes Kalaniho'okaha Cope Native Hawaiian Traditional Healing Center offers a range of traditional healing practices

with a council of elders overseeing the practices that take place alongside Western primary medical care.

• Southcentral Foundation in Anchorage, Alaska, is another integrative service where Alaska Natives are offered traditional healing as well as Western medicine within a range of wellness, trauma recovery, and lifestyle programmes.

• The Native American Health Center serves the Californian Bay area and extends its services to Native and non-Native Americans alike. As a community health centre they collaborate with other groups and organisations to promote the aims of rebuilding community, strengthening individuals, and restoring culture.

I will describe some foundations for Native American healing practices, but I want to highlight the importance of not making assumptions that there is a pan-indigenous way of looking at traditional healing and its practice as there are stark differences amongst the different regions and cultures.

Spirituality and culture are essential to healing as is the intimate link to relationships with elders and other cultural leaders. The healing process also goes beyond the individual and into their family, community, nation, and future generations. The individual has the main responsibility for their healing, and the healer is there to facilitate their process.

The Native American knowledge framework seems to be standing on the pillars of the spiritual, emotional, physical, and social realms of life which are seen as balanced in a holistic, inclusive, and respectful way.

Spiritual 'connectedness' is at the core of the Native American traditional healing. Being in harmony with the natural environment, meditating, praying, fasting, or using traditional medicine are the paths towards a strong physical body and mind.

In Navajo culture specifically, the *hataalii* performs the healing rituals and sees the person as a whole being with mind, body, and spirit and all those in connection to the other people, families, communities, the planet, and the universe. The purpose is for the individual in need to travel towards self-awareness and spiritual attunement that will then allow for oneness with Creation.

The rituals practised during traditional healing can be clustered into the following generic categories (with variations according to each culture and adaptations according to the context and resources):

- *Talking/healing circle*: the ancient version of the elders sitting in a circle can also be adapted for people in general sitting in a circle and listening deeply and speaking from the heart. A feather or talking stick is passed around in the circle, in a sunwise (clockwise) direction, and the holder is invited and encouraged to engage in some truthful speaking. The circle is a place of unconditional acceptance and non-interruption that provides healing and an opportunity for heart-truth. The ritual of the circle starts with a prayer by the traditional practitioner in charge.
- *Sweat lodge ceremony*: this takes place in dome-shaped structures used for purification and healing rites. The leader of the ritual guides the participants in prayer or song around the hot stones placed in the middle and whilst water is poured on the stones to create steam. It represents the womb of Mother Earth, and it is a sacred place where participants sweat out toxins and impurities and can ask for forgiveness, healing, hope, and vision.
- *Smudging:* in this ritual the four sacred plants (sage, sweetgrass, cedar, and tobacco) are ignited in a shell or small container. The smoke produced is then wafted around a person or space with a hand or eagle feather with the aim of cleansing them from negative thoughts and feelings, purifying the soul, and bringing clarity to the mind. At the end of the ceremony the ashes that represent the negative thoughts and feelings are disposed of on the bare soil.
- *Story-telling*
- *Songs and drumming*

Finally, the *Medicine Wheel/Sacred Hoop* is a symbolism used by various Native American tribes for generations now, and it symbolises the cycles of life and dimensions of health. Its actual embodiment is of the Four Directions, as well as Father Sky, Mother Earth, and Spirit Tree. Its ritual use involves movement in clockwise circular directions for the alignment of the forces of Nature.

Traditional healing within the Native American tribes is mainly based on the seasons as these can influence the practices on each occasion. The use of the surrounding land contributes to this cycle of seasons as alongside the previously described ceremonies, traditional healers also use plants, herbs, trees, soil, food, and water.

SOUTH AMERICA

Ecuador

Ecuador is a unique example of a country that has integrated traditional healing and medicine into its national health system since 1998. The 'Buen Vivir' plan (2009) also sought to incorporate the ancestral knowledge of healing as well as the experience of traditional healers into the formal health services.

The equivalent of the shaman in Ecuador is the *yachay* or *yachactaita* or *unwishin* or *visionario*. The focus for the achievement of health, when there is an ill element, is a balance between the physical, spiritual, social, and mental body, and all this goes alongside a consistent good diet and maintenance of balance and harmony.

The Quichua (Inca) people see health not just as the absence of pain and disease – emotional or physical – but mainly as the achievement of inner harmony and balance within the individual, the family, the community, nature, and the universe. Healing is inclusive and pluralistic and places humans into the universe.

In 1984 the two first Quichua people who graduated from medical school founded Jambihuasi (Health Care House) in North Ecuador. This was a unique community-based and culturally adapted service that brought together *yachactaitas* and Western trained medical professionals, who worked together with equality and mutual support for the best outcome for their patients. As a service it pioneered the idea of 'medical pluralism' given that patients (and their families) could choose what kind of practitioner they would like to see according to the kind of illness they felt they had. So, when a patient felt they were within the spectrum of Quichua illnesses – for example *rurashca* (witchcraft) or *mancharishca* (sudden fright caused by malign spirits) – they would see a *yachactaita* but when they experienced something more intense – for example psychotic episode – they would choose to see a medical doctor. The Jambihuasi service developed into the Runajambi (medicine of the Quichua people) Institute for the study of Quichua Culture and Health, where clinical work was combined with health education and promotion.

Peru

Unlike the previously mentioned individual powers of the shaman, in Peru shamanism belongs in the context of the tribe. The main reference for all practices is the community itself and the individual's needs and duties come second.

The role of traditional healers and medicinal plants are integral in the Peruvian traditional healthcare system. Traditional healing is multidimensional: the spiritual, environmental, and physical worlds interconnect as the body – and its health – is seen dependent on its relations to these three dimensions of being.

Spirit-based illnesses are believed to be the result of disrespect and abuse of the mother land (*Pachamama*) and traditional healers are responsible for their diagnosis (i.e. what spiritual agent causes the disease) and treatment.

Traditional healers in indigenous Peruvian communities are highly respected not only because of their knowledge but because of their role in disseminating the traditions, culture, and knowledge to the next generations.

Paraguay

For the indigenous people of Paraguay (with smaller groups in Argentina, Bolivia, and Brazil), the Guarani, there is a deep spiritual connection between the individual and their mental health. Similarly, a traditional healer needs to have a spiritual dream in order to pursue the route of healing. Any member of the community, irrespective of their age, can become a shaman. Their work is based on the understanding that health comes from the respect and embodiment of the harmonious relationship between the human and non-human, alongside the practising of living together and respecting the space of the other (*'Ka'aguy Porã*). Silence seems to be a common factor for health.

CONCLUSION AND THOUGHTS FOR THE FUTURE

After the introduction of Western medicine and psychological approaches into the global majority world through colonisation and its undermining and prohibiting policies towards traditional healing, we seem to still be talking about the impact of the cultural–ideological clash.

It has been mostly within high-income countries and settings that the role of traditional healers within the mental healthcare system has been researched (see Australia or New Zealand). The Partnership for Mental Health Development in Sub-Saharan Africa (PaM-D) is an exemption, bringing together traditional healers, primary healthcare workers, and service users across Ghana, Kenya, and Nigeria. This project is a unique example of how psychotherapy can be seen from multiple perspectives and how there is the potential for collaborative shared care, without perpetuating the colonial trauma of superiority and excluding vital approaches to therapy.

Another contemporary example of therapy seen under the prism of culture and the mental health treatment gap in developing countries is Zimbabwe's 'Friendship Bench' project, conceived and developed by Dixon Chibanda. This is a combination of tradition and Western ideas of therapy. The healing aspect of listening is combined with the respect for the elders and their wisdom – especially the female matriarchs of families – and cognitive behavioural therapy. Clients visit designated benches that are seen as secure places outside the local clinics and where 'grandmas' act as listeners. 'Grandmas' act as custodians, but they are also trained in the previously mentioned approach so that they support their clients in a process of empowerment for problem solving on their own. The Friendship Bench project has been adopted also by Zambia, Kenya, and Malawi, as well as Kuwait, Jordan, and even New York City.

This thought takes us to the idea of *indigenisation* of therapy and the social and political movement in the mental health sector towards an *integrative model* of care and against the existing monocultural view of healing. With traditional healers negotiating a new space within the changing world, it feels more than vital to adopt Mi'kmaw Elders Albert's and Murdena Marshall's (from the teachings of Chief Charles Labrador of Acadia First Nation in Nova Scotia) 'two-eyed seeing' framework; we need to learn

> to see from one eye with the strengths of Indigenous knowledge and ways of knowing, and from the other eye with the strengths of mainstream knowledge and ways of knowing, and to use both these eyes together, for the benefit of all.
>
> (Asamoah et al., 2023: 23)

This more holistic bio-psycho-social-spiritual collaborative care model requires, of course, consent from both sides and a genuine and respectful engagement into this ongoing dialogue, based in equality and recognition of the power imbalance that cultural genocide brought throughout the history of colonialism.

Integration is reported to be already practised by China, Korea, and Vietnam and supported by Australia as we saw in the example I described earlier on in this chapter. It is a model that can address not only the worldwide mental health treatment gap but can also bring on the surface the necessity for *inter-culturality* in therapy. The latter is a process that supports consolidation of a more equitable and participatory socio-cultural system through different tools. It can be applied in the therapy field too, a completely different practice, of course, from the current tendency for *cultural appropriation*.

Considering the widespread call for balanced, holistic, and integrated approaches to therapy by First Nations peoples, it makes sense to pursue the previously mentioned therapy agenda for both indigenous and non-indigenous populations, healing in this way the cultural illness that leads to individual illness. It's about striving for a parity of approaches and reconnecting with different forms of wisdom, from which the disconnection has caused some general suffering that not many people acknowledge or perceive as so.

Have you ever explored/Do you know of any traditional healing practices in your culture?

What are your beliefs/biases/feelings around traditional healing practices that include the other than human and the need for connection of humans with their natural environment?

Have you ever felt any gap in your treatment of distress by the Western medicalised system for emotional/mental health?

RECOMMENDED READING

Incayawar, M., Wintrob, R., Bouchard, L., & Bartocci, G. (Eds.). (2009). *Psychiatrists and traditional healers: Unwitting partners in global mental health.* Chichester: Wiley-Blackwell.

Pham, T., Richav, K., Wainberg, M., & Kohrt, B. (2021). Reassessing the mental health treatment gap: What happens if we include the impact of traditional healing on mental illness? *Community Mental Health Journal, 57*(4), 777–791. https://doi.org/10.1007/s10597-020-00705-5

REFERENCES

Achan, G., Eni, R., Kinew, K., Phillips-Beck, W., Lavoie, J., & Katz, A. (2021). The two great healing traditions: Issues, opportunities, and recommendations for an integrated first nations healthcare system in Canada. *Health Systems and Reform*, *7*(1), e1943814. https://doi.org/10.1080/23288604.2021.1943814

Asamoah, G., Khakpour, M., Carr, T., & Groot, G. (2023). Exploring indigenous traditional healing programs in Canada, Australia, and New Zealand: A scoping review. *Explore*, *19*(1), 14–25. https://doi.org/10.1016/j.explore.2022.06.004

Bagge, N., & Berliner, P. (2021). Psychotherapy and indigenous people in the Kingdom of Denmark. *Psychotherapy and Politics International*, *19*(2), e1586. https://doi.org/10.1002/ppi.1586

Bodibe, R. C. (1992). Traditional healing: An indigenous approach to mental health problems. In J. Uys (Ed.), *Psychological counselling in the South African context* (pp. 149–165). Cape Town, South Africa: Maskew Miller Longman.

Crozier, S., & Pizzini, N. (2019). Engaging with indigenous knowledge to shape a bicultural counselling programme in Aotearoa New Zealand. *Psychotherapy and Politics International*, *18*(2), 1–21. https://doi.org/10.1002/ppi.1515

Durie, M. (1998). *Whaiora: Māori health and development* (2nd ed.). Melbourne, Australia: Oxford University Press.

Gureje, O., Nortje, G., Makanjuola, V., Oladeji, B., Seedat, S., & Jenkins, R. (2015). The role of global traditional and complementary systems of medicine in the treatment of mental health disorders. *Lancet Psychiatry*, *2*(2), 168–177. https://doi.org/10.1016/S2215-0366(15)00013-9

Hall, A., Poutu, M., & Wilson, C. (2012). Waka Oranga: The development of an indigenous professional organisation within a psychotherapeutic discourse in Aotearoa New Zealand. *Psychotherapy and Politics International*, *10*(1), 7–16. https://doi.org/10.1002/ppi.1255

Haque, I., Chowdhury, A., Shahjahan, M., & Harun, G. (2018). Traditional healing practices in rural Bangladesh: A qualitative investigation. *BMC Complementary and Alternative Medicine*, *18*, 62. https://doi.org/10.1186/s12906-018-2129-5

Kapur, R. (1979). The role of traditional healers in mental health care in rural India. *Social Sciences & Medicine, Part B: Medical Anthropology*, *13*(1), 27–31. https://doi.org/10.1016/0160-7987(79)90015-2

Koithan, M., & Farrell, C. (2010). Indigenous native American healing traditions. *The Journal for Nurse Practitioners*, *6*(6), 477–478. https://doi.org/10.1016/j.nurpra.2010.03.016

Laplanche, J., & Pontalis, J. B. (1967/1988). *The language of psycho-analysis*. London: Karnac.

MacLeod, S. (2014). Immrama: Journeys in indigenous Celtic shamanic practice. *A Journal of Contemporary Shamanism*, *7*(1), 28–34.

Mahood, K. (2018). The man in the log: Tjukurpa wati minyma kutjaratjara. *The Monthly (Australia)*, 8.

Mathibela, M., Egan, B., Du Plessis, H., & Potgieter, M. (2015). Socio-cultural profile of Bapedi traditional healers as indigenous knowledge custodians and conservation partners in the Blouberg area, Limpopo Province, South Africa. *Journal of Ethnobiology and Ethnomedicine*, 11, 49. https://doi.org/10.1186/s13002-015-0025-3

McKendrick, J., Brooks, R., Hudson, J., Thorpe, M., & Bennett, P. (2013). *Aboriginal and Torres Strait Islander healing programs: A literature review*. Canberra, Australia: The Healing Foundation.

Montenegro, R., & Stephens, C. (2006). Indigenous health in Latin America and the Caribbean. *Lancet*, 367, 1859–1869. https://doi.org/10.1016/S0140-6736(06)68808-9

Montiel Tafur, M., Crowe, T., & Torres, E. (2009). A review of curanderismo and healing practices among Mexicans and Mexican Americans. *Occupational Therapy International*, 16(1), 82–88. https://doi.org/10.1002/oti.265

Naka, K., Toguchi, S., Takaishi, T., Ishizu, H., & Sasaki, Y. (1985). Yuta (Shaman) and community mental health on Okinawa. *International Journal of Social Psychiatry*, 31(4), 267–274. https://doi.org/10.1177/002076408503100404

Ngaanyatjarra Pitjantjatjara Yankunytjatjara Women's Council Aboriginal Corporation. (2013). *Ngangkari: Traditional Aboriginal healers*. Alice Springs, Australia: Ngaanyatjarra Pitjantjatjara Yankunytjatjara Women's Council Aboriginal Corporation.

Ngoma, M. C., Prince, M., & Mann, A. (2003). Common mental disorders among those attending primary health clinics and traditional healers in urban Tanzania. *British Journal of Psychiatry*, 183, 349–355. https://doi.org/10.1192/bjp.183.4.349

Peeters, L. (2010). The Marumali program: An aboriginal model of healing. In N. Purdie, P. Dudgeon & R. Walker (Eds.), *Working together: Aboriginal and Torres Strait Islander mental health and wellbeing principles and practice* (pp. 287–292). Canberra, Australia: Australian Government Department of Health and Ageing.

Portman, T., & Garrett, M. (2006). Native American healing traditions. *International Journal of Disability, Development and Education*, 53(4), 453–469. https://doi.org/10.1080/10349120601008647

Rivera, E. (2005). Espiritismo: The flywheel of the Puerto Rican spiritual traditions. *Interamerican Journal of Psychology*, 39(2), 295–300.

Ryoko, S. (2014). *A society accepting of spirit possession: Mental health and shamanism in Okinawa*. London: Routledge.

San Roque, C. (2012). Aranke, or in the long line: Reflections on the 2011 Sigmund Freud award for psychotherapy and the lineage of traditional indigenous therapy in Australia. *Psychotherapy and Politics International*, 10(2), 93–104. https://doi.org/10.1002/ppi.1262

Schouler-Ocak, M., & Kastrup, M. (Eds.). (2020). *Intercultural psychotherapy for immigrants, refugees, asylum seekers and ethnic minority patients.* New York: SpringerLink.

Shange, S., & Ross, E. (2022). "The question is not how but why things happen": South African traditional healers explanatory model of mental illness, its diagnosis and treatment. *Journal of Cross-Cultural Psychology*, *53*(5). 503–521. https://doi.org/10.1177/00220221221077361

Shankar, B., Saravanan, B., & Jacob, K. (2006). Explanatory models of common mental disorders among traditional healers and their patients in rural South India. *International Journal of Social Psychiatry*, *52*(3), 221–233. https://doi.org/10.1177/0020764006067215

Shimoji, A. (1992). Interface between shamanism and psychiatry in Miyako Islands, Okinawa, Japan: A viewpoint from medical and psychiatric anthropology. *The Japanese Journal of Psychiatry and Neurology*, *45*(4), 767–774. https://doi.org/10.1111/j.1440-1819.1991.tb00515.x

Solera-Deuchar, L., Mussa, M., Ali, S., Haji, H., & McGovern, P. (2020). Establishing views of traditional healers and biomedical practitioners on collaboration in mental health care in Zanzibar: A qualitative pilot study. *International Journal of Mental Health Systems*, *14*(1), 1–10. https://doi.org/10.1186/s13033-020-0336-1

Tudor, K. (Ed.). (2011). *The turning tide: Pluralism and partnership in psychotherapy in Aotearoa New Zealand.* Auckland, Aotearoa New Zealand: LC Publications.

Waldram, J. (Ed.). (2008). *Aboriginal healing in Canada: Studies in therapeutic meaning and practice.* Ottawa, Canada: Aboriginal Healing Foundation.

Walter, M., & Fridman, E. (Eds.). (2004). *Shamanism: An encyclopedia of world beliefs, practices and culture.* Santa Barbara, CA: ABC-CLIO.

WHO. (2002). *WHO traditional medicine strategy 2002–2005.* World Health Organization.

WHO. (2013). *Mental health action plan 2013–2020.* World Health Organization.

Wolff, R. (2014). The effects of integrative healthcare on Peruvian Indigenous groups. *Studies by Undergraduate Researchers at Guelph*, *7*(2), 5–12.

Wood, H. (unknown date). Healing in the Celtic world. In S. Clancy & F. Nicholson (Eds.), *Land, sea and sky.* Online Book.

Yen, J., & Wilbraham, L. (2003). Discourses of culture and illness in South African mental health care and indigenous healing, Part I: Western psychiatric power. *Transcultural Psychiatry*, *40*(4), 542–561. https://doi.org/10.1177/1363461503404005

2

PSYCHOANALYSIS AND THE PSYCHODYNAMIC UMBRELLA
A FAMILY WITH MANY CHILDREN

What three words come to mind when you hear the word 'psychoanalysis'?
How often do you use the words 'unconscious', 'defence', 'narcissistic' when talking about relationships, other people, or yourself?

Psychoanalysis can be defined as a branch of psychotherapy that focuses on the development of the mind–body as this is influenced by childhood experiences. It is grounded in the belief in the unconscious, and all the mental phenomena that this produces, and in practice it pays close attention to *transference* and *countertransference*, two processes that have become vital for the work of contemporary psychoanalysts.

There are two dimensions to hold in mind when considering the classification of psychoanalytic models as we will explore them in this chapter:

(1) Balance between environmental or intra-psychic factors in the development of the personality
(2) Emphasis on causation and mechanism in approaching mental phenomena, or on understanding and meaning-making

DOI: 10.4324/9780367824334-3

Despite the ongoing criticism of psychoanalysis as a gloomy theory, it is important to remember that there have always been some psychoanalytic theorists who were optimistic about human nature and focused on the individual capacity and desire to reach one's potential (e.g. Anna Freud, Adler, and Horney).

In this chapter only I will refer to the dyad therapist–client as analyst–patient, keeping in line with the terminology used by psychoanalysts. Some other differences of psychoanalysis in comparison to other psychotherapeutic approaches are the frequency of sessions (i.e. more than once per week) and the use of the couch for the patient who lies down and the analyst sits on a chair behind them. This latter point was argued against even by some of Freud's students, so it has changed over the years and the set up now resembles what all other therapies offer (i.e. two facing-each-other chairs), but there are still some classical psychoanalysts who work in this way.

SIGMUND FREUD: THE FATHER OF PSYCHOANALYSIS AND HIS THEORIES

Sigmund Freud holds a very special place in collective fantasies, and his recognition spans from pop culture to avant-garde art. He is the man associated with the birth of psychotherapy, as this is practised in the Western world, with the use of the couch and the talking cure. But how did it all start?

Freud was born during the industrial revolution (1856) and grew up in Vienna, one of the most prosperous centres of the 'civilised' world. His background, though, was not characterised by privilege, and his Jewish heritage put several barriers at the beginning of his career given the rising anti-semitic climate in Europe. His life and the historical period within which he developed his theories inevitably influenced his thinking and the way he saw the world.

Although Freud's career started with hypnosis, he soon developed his own take on this well-established method and concentrated on creating a more tangible and scientific approach. He was, after all, interested in proving his approach and following the scientific paradigm. As we will see from his theories, there is a strong influence from archaeology which we see in the image of excavating to find out the truth or reveal the past. A quick search on the internet will give you images of his practice rooms with the many artifacts he collected from ancient civilisations (see also his frequent use of words from the ancient Greek language – e.g. *Eros, Thanatos* – and concepts from Greek mythology – e.g. *Oedipal complex*).

Freud was part of the patriarchal and hierarchical society of his time. He tried, however, to take women's feelings seriously and not treat them simply as 'hysterics' which was the main trend when psychoanalysis was emerging as a new discipline. He initially put more emphasis on environmental factors and later saw the internal world as primary and he made the idea of conflict, over unacceptable aspects of the self, central to his work. His prolific writing started with the *Studies on Hysteria* which he co-authored with Josef Breuer in 1895.

Initial ideas and approach to hysteria

According to Breuer and Freud, hysteria was caused by trapped memories and the feelings associated with them. Those memories and feelings had never been lived through in an ordinary way. Therefore, they had become split off from the rest of the mind, and they festered and rose to the surface in the form of disconcerting and seemingly inexplicable symptoms. If those symptoms were traced to their origins, their meanings would become apparent and the feelings would be discharged in a cathartic burst; the result would be the disappearance of symptoms.

Certain experiences generate feelings that become dissociated, split off from the rest of the mind because the actual content of those memories and feelings was disturbing, unacceptable, and in conflict with the rest of the person's ideas and feelings. In other words, those memories and feelings were incompatible with the rest of consciousness and were therefore actively kept out of awareness – from themselves as well as from others.

Free association was a term and process that Freud introduced as an alternative to hypnosis. It is a learned and not an imposed method according to which the patient is encouraged to say anything that comes to their mind. The analyst encourages the patient to share all thoughts that cross their minds, with the hope of tackling the filtering out of conflictual content that happens in the everyday conscious process of talking. Because the patient is fully awake (unlike when in a hypnotised state), they can be shown that what they share unintentionally, contains disguised ideas and feelings that they have been keeping out of awareness. Freud believed that hysteria was a disease not of the brain but of the mind; he believed that it was ideas, not nerves, that were the source of trouble. According to his *Seduction Theory*, a repressed memory of an early sexual trauma was at the root of hysteria and obsessional neurosis. Freud believed his patients were relating true, factual stories around their early sexual abuse.

For several reasons – a combination of personal explorations and societal pressure – Freud reviewed this theory in 1896 and he postulated that the memories of sexual abuse were, in fact, imaginary fantasies, memories of wishes, and longings. This is his *theory of infantile sexuality and instinctual drive*, with its *erogenous zones* and psychosexual stages (oral, anal, phallic-oedipal, latent, and genital) that changed the way babies and children are seen even today.

Here I would like to introduce you to the widely used term of *Oedipal complex* that stems from Greek mythology (and Sophocles's ancient Greek tragedy *Oedipus Rex*). The myth features the king of Thebes who fulfilled a prophecy that he would kill his father and marry his mother. In Freud's work the *Oedipal complex* becomes a powerful and sometimes overwhelming drama in a child's life, with no easy resolution: the aim of all the child's desires becomes genital intercourse with the parent of the opposite sex. The parent of the same sex becomes a dangerous, feared rival, and the only way forward is for the child to identify with them and maintain some sort of ambivalence towards them, loving and hating them.

Moving towards the two models of the mind

As Freud shifted his clinical task from the discovery of his hypnotised patients' secrets to the removal of the defences against those secrets, he also tried to understand the mind in the form of a shape. His 1900 *Topographical Model* resembled an iceberg floating in the sea: the *conscious* part is the tip of the iceberg sticking out of the water, the *preconscious* part is towards the edge of the water, and the *unconscious* part is deeper in the water and holds the biggest part of the iceberg.

More specifically:

• The conscious part contains those ideas and feelings in awareness at any particular time

- The preconscious part contains acceptable ideas and feelings that are capable of becoming conscious, like a reservoir of accessible thoughts and memories and a censor, capable of modifying instinctual wishes of the system unconscious
- The unconscious part contains unacceptable ideas and feelings; it's about those aspects of ourselves which conflict with consciously held ideals and, as a result, may be denied, suppressed, or disowned

The reason behind the very existence of the unconscious is the *pleasure principle*, which is what humans and animals have in common. The pleasure principle is about our drive to derive pleasure and to preserve our life force. This drive tends to be stronger than any consideration for other people and their wishes. It is a preservation instinct which can also be seen as a threat to society and civilisation which expects people to put the wider good above their own self-interest. Therefore, the pleasure principle has to be repressed, a process learnt from when an infant is born.

Freud saw dreams as *'The royal road to the unconscious', 'The disguised fulfilment of a repressed wish'*, and we can understand that as the demands of adaptation to a world with certain conditions are relaxed, a clearer picture of the inner world emerges. That's why he believed in the power of interpretation as a means of reaching the psychological meaning of dreams.

In 1923 Freud shifted his model into a form with parts, where instinctual wishes became more central. The *Structural Model* is concerned with how individual personalities are structured as adaptations to the demands of the instinctual wishes, with much consideration though of the external reality at the same time. So, the focus is on all those hidden energy factors as well as on the contradictions and discrepancies in one's agency when they have to navigate their development between their instinctual wishes and their external reality. This creates the following parts of the mind:

- *Superego*: the 'ego ideal', with all its conscience and ideals as a result of continuous internalisation of authority figures and cultural influences from very early in one's life. It is formed both from reality and fantasy, and its effects are experienced both consciously and unconsciously.

- *Ego*: the more rational, reality-oriented part (partly conscious, partly unconscious) with its main task being to control the more primitive id impulses and to balance those with the *reality principle*, alongside moderating the demands that come from the superego. This is a demanding and continuous process of keeping the three elements – external world and reality, id, and superego – in harmony.
- *Id*: the equivalent of the unconscious in the sense that it functions according to a more primary process of thinking and feeling.

The intention of analysis is, therefore, the strengthening of the ego, so that it can be in touch with fresher elements from the id whilst experiencing greater independence from the superego.

Conflict, adaptation, the principles, and the drives

As mentioned earlier, Freud put special emphasis on the idea of the inner conflict: instinctual wishes (see pleasure principle) are in opposition with the demands of reality (see reality principle); therefore, *defence mechanisms* are mobilised and cause delays or modifications of the expression of the instinctual wishes by the time those reach the conscious, and thus the individual experiences inner conflict.

Instinctual wishes – or tensions – are discharged through *objects* that are mainly the target of instinctual impulses. An object can be a person or something inanimate. The mother's breast and the mother herself is an object through which the infant's instincts achieve their aims (e.g. hunger or safety). Similarly for an adult with a shoe fetish, the shoe is a libidinal object that allows the expression of their sexual impulses. Objects in general symbolise someone/something significant for an individual's emotional world.

In the actual analysis of an individual we can see the inner conflict demonstrated in the conflict between past and present, between the inner child and the functioning adult. What seemed to not make sense for Freud, though, was the repetition of something painful that did not fit in well with the pleasure principle and its *life drive* or *Eros*. He also noticed that it was also more of an irrational act which frequently led to destruction. Therefore, he concluded there is another instinctual force that opposes the pleasure principle, the *death drive* or *Thanatos*. The drives are located in the id and are the force behind all mental life. They are also not separate from each other; they are in a state of perpetual fusion from the start of life.

Freud also saw the infant as *omnipotent* in their sense of being, and he believed that they initially direct their libidinal energy/libido towards themselves (*primary narcissism*). The next stage in an infant's development is to direct their libido externally and onto an object, for example mother or father. *Secondary narcissism* develops either as a defence or as an attitude when the individual tries to deny that they have lost the *introjected* objects (i.e. the imagined objects inside), and they replace the relationship with these introjected objects with an object outside the individual.

Transference and countertransference

Although these two terms have attracted so much attention for their definition within the psychoanalytic community, it is very interesting to notice their use in everyday language and popular culture.

Have you caught yourself behaving towards a friend/romantic partner as you would with your mother/father/primary caregiver?
　　Do you sometimes have a weird feeling or sensation when someone talks to you and you are puzzled about where that weird feeling/sensation came from?

Transference

This is a process where the patient transfers onto their analyst strong feelings and/or past experiences that were lived before with the important others in their life. The patient's internal drama is re-enacted with their analyst but in a new form rather than in pure repetition.

Freud initially saw transference as an unwanted obstacle in the memory work he endeavoured to do with his patients. As he experienced, though, the actual dynamics with his patients, he saw the importance of his patients' transferential feelings in accessing all that was repressed from childhood.

The analyst's role is to spot when transference happens so that they have a better insight into their patient's embodied history and previous relationships. The next step would be to help the patient make connections between current feelings and past experiences, as well as to accept those feelings as a product of a history when at some point they were understandable and appropriate.

The challenge for the analyst is to disidentify from the transference and to not act out according to the feeling that has been transferred onto them but make an interpretation that helps the patient to validate their feelings and to understand them in the context of their analysis. In this way a new needed relationship can develop, and the patient can, consequently, evolve new psychological capacities.

Countertransference

Freud's definition of countertransference was of the analyst's transference towards the patient; the first's own displaced past projected into the analytic situation. He saw it as an analyst-derived process that hinders and intrudes upon the analytic process and should be worked on in the analyst's own analysis.

Later on, the object relations school in Britain and the interpersonalists in the USA pushed the limits of the definition of countertransference and highlighted its importance in advancing the analytic work. It was in 1950 and in Paula Heimann's seminal paper on countertransference that we can see how the subjective feelings of the analyst can be used as guidance about the internal world of the patient; in other words, countertransference is seen as a specific response to the patient and the material they bring to the relationship. This development has seen further explorations and definitions regarding possible somatic responses the analyst might have (*somatic countertransference*), roles they might feel they take (*embodied countertransference*), or even movement repertoire and gestures and postures (*kinetic countertransference*).

The more contemporary definition with its emphasis on the interactional nature of the phenomenon of countertransference is an example of the dismantling of authoritarianism in psychoanalysis.

In practice, the analyst needs to go through some thorough self-scrutiny when working with countertransferential material to exclude potential personal material. The several schools within the psychoanalytic tradition utilise countertransference in different ways: some choose to only recognise but not share the analyst's feelings/embodied and somatic experience, and others use *disclosure* to process with the patient the material shared in the bipersonal-intersubjective field.

LES ENFANTS TERRIBLES THAT DISAPPOINTED THE 'FATHER': JUNG, ADLER, FERENCZI, AND RANK

Freud developed close relationships with a handful of his students for whom he had high expectations of continuing his vision. But like a father who wants to maintain the ties with (or control . . .) his children, he could not accept any deviations from his original theory and therefore one after the other, members of his original circle of protégés argued with him and consequently left his circle, or they were expelled. These 'enfants terribles' created their own schools of psychoanalytic thinking and practice, and we will be looking at the main points of their theories next. The title of this section comes from Jean Cocteau's 1929 same name novel that inspired a movie, an opera, and several performances; I have used it to emphasise the intensity of the splits, as if they took place in a theatre play.

CARL GUSTAV JUNG AND ANALYTICAL PSYCHOLOGY

One of the very first protégées to split from Freud, Carl Gustav Jung was seen as Freud's intellectual son and the successor to his 'throne'. Jung's practices, though (e.g. face-to-face encounters or getting involved with his patients) and his fascination with mysticism and the occult made Freud uncomfortable and in the end Jung's theoretical deviations created an irreparable schism between the two men.

Jung's focus on the role of symbolic experiences in human life, his belief in an inherent positive tendency for self-realisation, and an overall importance placed on the interrelation of psyche and body framed the development of his theory and practice in a unique way. His approach is known as *analytical psychology*.

Theory of personality development and psychopathology

Jung's most influential theoretical contribution is his *character typology* classification where he placed individual personality differences in (1) the way we perceive internal and external stimuli (*functions: sensation, intuition*, *thinking*, and *feeling*), and (2) the way we orientate our libidinal movement (*attitudes: introversion-extroversion* and the scale ranging between them).

Jung saw personality development as dependent on instincts and the past – following Freud's ideas here – but he also highlighted the significance of the present. He postulated that *psychic energy* is the source of power for mental activity. Since he rejected Freud's emphasis on sexuality, we can see psychic energy as a more neutral term for *libido*. Psychic energy attracts clusters of ideas (*complexes*) that are related, emotionally charged, and a means of expression for the psyche.

Although Jung never defined certain developmental stages, he saw a clear distinction between youth and middle age, as well as a gradual separate development of the following entities:

- *Consciousness*: as in the original Freudian theory, consciousness is seen as the tip of the iceberg, with the ego at its centre – given that the ego constitutes the centre of our awareness. Within one's consciousness we can also find *the persona*, the façade that protects us from the demands of society when it's hard to confront the world with our true inner feelings.
- *Personal unconscious*: this entity is formed from birth and contains material from personal experience that is either not yet or no longer at the level of awareness. The *shadow* lies in here, and it represents and consists of all the unwanted by the ego and repressed material. The shadow is also seen as the container of shameful and unpleasant feelings.
- *Collective unconscious*: this is the ancestral reservoir of *archetypes* (i.e. primordial images) that a newborn baby carries in their psyche. The archetypes (e.g. the mother, the hero, the trickster), Jung believed, are universal thought forms and emotions that have been created by humanity's repeated experiences, and they condition us to look at the world in certain ways. The *animus* is the inner masculine image in a woman, and the *anima* is the inner female archetype in a man. *Anima* and *animus* can define either compensatory or balancing dimensions of gender and sexual identity.

Jung's theory of personality is very much focused on synthesising opposites as he saw opposites as the central preconditions of psychic life – see previously mentioned anima-animus but also psyche-soma and instinct-image. *Psyche* here is seen as a self-regulating entity, whilst the *Self* (with capital S) gives the sense of order in the psyche as it serves as the new centre of the personality. As the ultimate goal of personality development, Self also has the capacity to mediate the opposites and facilitate the process of achieving wholeness (*individuation*).

Psychological disturbance is seen as associated with both the personal and collective unconscious and as a demonstration of the individual's difficulty in interacting with both the inner world of the psyche and the environment in a free and autonomous way.

Practice, aims, and emphases

Jung continued the tradition of dream interpretation and saw dreams as expressions of the psyche through the use of symbols. He also used *active imagination* – a form of meditative practice that could take expressive form such as painting, drawing, writing, dance, or conducting inner dialogue – as another means for the emergence of *symbolism*. Symbolism was central in Jung's understanding of the integration of the psyche as he saw it as the facilitator for uniting the conscious and the unconscious (*transcendent function*).

The aim of analytical psychology is for the individual to explore the unfolding of their inherent and unique personality. This is the difficult and complicated journey of self-discovery called *individuation*. Individuation is also characterised by its spirituality as the individual experiences the process of listening to and being guided by the Self.

Other emphases in analytical psychology include Jung's view of bodies as shadow-holders, as holders of the unexpressed aspects of the Self and as the originators of symbols. Also, Jung's legacy has left behind the concept of *synchronicity* (i.e. events that are related to each other but in a meaningful coincidence rather than by cause and effect) which is widely used in today's everyday language too.

ALFRED ADLER AND INDIVIDUAL PSYCHOLOGY

Adler's position within the psychoanalytic circles was of the theorist who stressed the dynamics of power in personality development, relationships, and within the analytic process. He was especially sympathetic to socialism and endeavoured with his theory and practice to foster conditions of greater equality. An example of this was his 1918 famous free Child Guidance Clinics in the Red Vienna of Social Democrats that treated children in the company of their parents – a project that influenced child-rearing approaches all the way to New York and Harlem. His social and preventive psychological view expanded through the development of day hospitals and therapeutic clubs for working class people. It is noticeable, also, that he had expressed opinions about gender equality – how it is necessary for societies to correct the process of *masculine protests* in women, meaning that unconscious desire in women and girls to be male as a reaction to their inferior position in society.

Adler's view of human beings was that we do create our world and that we have agency. This was contradictory to Freud's theory on unconscious motivation and thinking in causality terms (i.e. people doing things 'because of'). Adler focused on *ego instincts*, those conscious willed behaviours that lead to actions 'in order to'. Another deviation was his emphasis on social factors that made him also disagree with Freud's view of instincts. He did not ascribe to the notion of the inevitability of innate instinctual urges and believed in the active engagement of individuals in selecting their fundamental life goals and the means of achieving them.

The centrality of relationships in personality development and neurosis

Adler refused to see humans as isolated beings and was interested in the interaction of the individual with society, as well as between individuals in groups. He saw individual striving as a process that aims for relationships and that relationship failure leads to neurosis. The latter, he postulated, has its origins in the attempts to deal with feelings of inferiority (physical or emotional) that are channelled into a compensatory drive to power.

For Adler, human beings have an innate potential for relating to others that creates a sense of kinship within humanity, and therefore allows for survival through cooperation. We see here how Adler left behind him the psychoanalytic pre-occupation with intra-psychic phenomena and concentrated on a more social view of humans, where social factors and community – rather than Freud's superego or Jung's collective unconscious – are important and formative for personality development.

Individual psychology

This is Adler's main body of theory and approach and one that can be characterised as a social psychology since it sees co-existence and co-living in this world as a need for the survival of fully functioning individuals. It is an approach based on the notion of 'me with you', of social interest as the motivation for reaching one's potential; in Adler's words '*the individual becomes an individual only in a social context*'.

In individual psychology all behaviour is seen as purposive and an individual as being what they believe; one's belief system is held out of their awareness, and it includes their feelings, behaviour, and conscious thoughts. Part of life's mission is to discover the purpose of the joint – and not conflicted – efforts of the conscious and the unconscious. Change, therefore, happens by shifting the way one experiences life (see perception of the self, the others, and the world) rather than focusing on life per se.

A child's position in the family constellation is very important in Adler's approach. He saw, though, the effect of birth order only as a tendency rather than as a certainty. From this idea he started exploring the process of *striving for superiority* and the concept of *inferiority complex*. According to Adler, human behaviour aims primarily for self-perfection. If in that process there is a feeling of inferiority, on a pathological level, that dominates the individual, an overwhelming sense of inadequacy that restrains development, then we can see the inferiority complex in action. These exaggerated feelings of weakness can also paralyse the ability to consider ways of overcoming one's difficulties and are usually accompanied by a conscious or unconscious *superiority complex*, creating a sense of confusion in the individual who vacillates between the two extremes. Adler saw sexual behaviour as another form of striving for superiority. The latter never stops as it is an essential process to the mind and sets life in motion.

A balanced view of this striving is when it is channelled towards social interests. On the other hand, psychopathology in this approach is seen as a misguided style of life that lacks connections with social interests.

Another important contribution of Adler's work was his correlation between mental tension and body language. He paid attention and explored body language as an expression of lifestyle and character traits and encouraged the use of expressive movement.

SÀNDOR FERENCZI AND THE CONCEPT OF EMPATHY IN ACTIVE THERAPY

Ferenczi is seen as the founder of all relationship-based psychoanalytic approaches and one of the most theoretically and clinically innovative of Freud's early disciples. He was also known as the master of difficult cases as he extended therapy to patients with more severe symptomatology and even psychosis. His thinking, writing, and clinical experimentation were characterised by a radical relational quality that shook up the constraints that Freud's psychoanalysis was posing at the time. In that way, we can see Ferenczi's influence in the later developments of Interpersonal Psychoanalysis and Object Relations theories. He deviated from Freud's theory in a tangible way as he put emphasis on emotions, rather than ideas, on external trauma vs. internal drives, and he also shifted the attention from the existing individual blame for symptoms to dyadic concepts. Overall, he highlighted the importance of love more than libido and shaped his theories of love and trauma accordingly.

Ferenczi's radical way of being within psychoanalysis was depicted in his political devotion to social change, and he saw psychoanalysis as a vehicle for social and political transformation.

Active therapy and its rectifying good experience

Ferenczi's exceptional empathy for human suffering distinguished him from the then held back attitude promoted within the psychoanalytic circles. For him, the analyst required a *certain passion*, a more emotive role in the therapeutic relationship, and this is what he saw as the root to cultivating transferential dynamics.

The therapeutic relationship, in Ferenczi's approach, can be a rectifying good experience for those patients who have suffered from trauma, neglect, or deprivation. He believed in the power and emotionally corrective experience of warmth and love and even offered his patients physical holding as a form of emotional regulation. His approach, therefore, was more interactive than what had existed thus far, and he also encouraged his patients to re-enact memories and fantasies, whilst he himself actively engaged in their process. This is also depicted in his understanding of the dynamic of transference and countertransference as a two-way process.

This more active and emotive participation in the analytic work gave Ferenczi the space to consider and experiment – briefly – with the idea of *mutual analysis* where analysts and patients would take turns in lying on the couch and free-associating.

His objections to the more detached observing role of the analyst extended also to the hierarchical and authoritarian nature of the existing practice. Ferenczi wanted to acknowledge his shortcomings to his patients, rather than expecting his interpretations to be received by the patient with no question.

Bioanalysis and the body as biological unconscious

One of Ferenczi's important contributions was the metaphor of the sea (*thalassa*) in his theory of genitality. His view of the body as the biological unconscious had an impact on how he saw the differentiation of the baby from the caregiver and the subsequent cravings for reconnection as both an inter- and intra-corporeal dynamic. *Bioanalysis* describes that tendency in every human to return to their intra-uterine experience, before the detrimental first inhaling of oxygen – after the passing from the liquid foetal environment to the aerobic respiration – transforms everything forever.

The interpersonal basis of trauma and the confusion of tongues

A major deviation from Freud was Ferenczi's strong believing of his patients and their history of childhood sexual abuse. He saw their symptoms and neuroses as the result of actual incidents and not as some sort of instinctually based fantasy. He defined trauma as an event that happens between an adult and a child and which has direct consequences on the latter's development of narcissism and the general structure of their ego and defence mechanisms. As an externally originated event, trauma also has an effect on the individual's memory as they use the mechanisms of splitting and fragmentation to cope with their emotional turmoil and their life.

We could see the formation of trauma in the following sequence of events and emotional processes: something happens and the trusted adult turns into an aggressor that destroys the child's security → intense fear paralyses the child → in order to survive, the child identifies with the aggressor who has now become an intra-psychic entity → the paradox of the child wishing to gratify the attacker → this allows the child to maintain a good image of the adult and continue with things as they were before → the adult's sense of guilt is introjected by the child → therefore, they feel that their act deserves punishment → splitting has already happened – the child feels both innocent and guilty at the same time → confusion between the memory of the events and the wish that nothing has happened. The adult's response plays, of course, an important role in the generation of trauma.

Ferenczi saw that in the previously described process something else also happens; there is a *confusion of tongues*. That is the confusion of language of love or tenderness that adults use versus the one a child uses. For the first tenderness is expressed in sexual forms, whilst for the latter tenderness is being met with maternal love that is neither overbearing nor neglectful. Thus, the confusion lies in the language of seduction.

The term *identification with the aggressor* is a vivid descriptor of the impact of trauma with its long-term emotional and intellectual consequences. Ferenczi placed special emphasis on early and/or chronic trauma and its impact on personality development and saw the importance of a warm empathic therapeutic relationship for the amelioration of the trauma conditioning.

Ferenczi's legacy extends into the speeding up of the analytic process to make it more widely available. He also redefined the ending of analysis as a conclusion of the experience of the unconscious, rather than a decision made by the analyst on behalf of the patient. He was, overall, active in the democratisation of psychoanalytic theory, practice, and the functioning of the psychoanalytic societies as professional organisations.

OTTO RANK AND THE 'HERE AND NOW'

Alongside Ferenczi, Rank was the first psychoanalyst to propose an *active therapy*, where the therapist was encouraged to see what was justified by the *here and now* – a term he coined – and what belonged to infantile material from the regressed client. In his view of an active therapy he also saw the importance of the client's emotional experience over some intellectual insight. Despite his extensive writings and strong influence in psychoanalysis and, even, humanistic psychotherapy, there is no school of 'Rankian' therapy as Rank himself was against specific ideologies and he wanted to move beyond psychoanalysis. In his relational and expressive approach to therapy, all feelings are grounded in the present and the client goes through a process of unlearning self-destructive ways of being and then learning more creative ones. Rank's image of the therapist is a collaborative and creative one, a figure who encourages new experiences in the therapeutic process. His overall emphasis was on encouraging clients to live life fully, with all its pain, and to learn to be beyond the limitations of death. He also saw the social order and the individual as interconnected; neither is in isolation of each other nor in absolute opposition.

Birth trauma, eternal anxiety, and seeking for a bounded self

Rank's view of the baby's sudden experience of being removed from the protecting environment of the womb during birth was that it was the first trauma people experience in life, and one that colours all the later experiences of anxiety. Thus, he believed, many clients seek to re-experience their birth as they seek to go through that developmental process that would allow them to consolidate a sense of a bounded self that is differentiated from the primary (m)other. Rank, therefore, postulated that the aim of therapy is exactly this: the repetition of the birth trauma but within the helpful framework of the therapeutic relationship where the therapist is experienced as a midwife through the process of transference and the client detaches themselves from the primal mother fixation.

For Rank there is a direct connection between the repetition of the birth trauma, the claim of the lost intra-uterus paradise and the whole circle of human creation; the latter includes fantasies, myths, the arts, philosophy, revolutions, as well as neurotic and psychotic symptoms.

Part of this pioneering view of human anxiety is Rank's theory of 'The Genesis of Object Relation' which preceded the school of Object Relations (see further down in this chapter) by some decades. He saw human development as a lifelong journey that involves continual negotiations between the individual with his objects, of the dual yearning for separation and connection.

Within the category of negotiations, we can also find Rank's notion of the *heroic myths* as wishful fantasies in childhood. Here the child has to negotiate with their inevitable disappointment towards their parents, when the former realise that the latter are no longer idealised. The *vanishing of happy times* and this traumatic disillusionment push the child to shrink into fantasy images of a grandiose self.

The will and personality development

The *will* is a central concept in Rank's theory and is connected to his long-term study of the creative personality and the general creative aspect of behaviour. It is the inner striving for self-differentiation and personal freedom, the dynamic organisation of one's personality for the achievement of some objective, and sometimes it links to the human quest for immortality.

A special characteristic of this concept is that it emphasises the active, integrative, and creative aspects of behaviour that promote active self-expression and a sense of control over necessary adjustments; a completely opposite to Freud's view of the passive, negative, and determinist aspects of personality development with all the despair towards the blind forces in life. Rank believed in the task of therapy as one of positive will organisation and mobilisation – will is a necessary corrective in the therapeutic process.

Alongside the will there are two more organising principles: *inhibition* and *impulse*. Inhibition for Rank is a basic and increasingly autonomous internal process that when it becomes more conscious, it turns into *denial*. Both inhibition and denial are negative will expressions which can be transformed into positive ones through therapy. *Impulse* is the dynamic aspect of will and not something connected to instincts and their biological orientation as in Freud's theory.

Rank also connected these three organising principles to three personality types that represent individuals that are not well adjusted according to a 'normal' standard, and their functioning in relationships and in life is marked by an imbalance within their set of organising principles:

- The creative type (see artists): for them will is predominant compared to the other two organising principles
- The neurotic type: they are dominated by inhibition
- The anti-social type: impulse is their main principle

In terms of the actual practice, Rank advocated each client's uniqueness and therefore an individualised and context-dependent approach that considers the broader universal concerns that make humans suffer. For him, therapy needed to be an active encounter and an opportunity to creatively overcome any inhibitions that prevent the individual from living life fully. Experiencing and the emotional dynamics in the actual therapeutic relationship were determining aspects of his process.

Finally, Rank seemed to have concerns over the extensive period of one's therapy and he set a time limit, with the view of an ending, as well as working on the important problem of separation.

ANNA FREUD, THE EGO, ITS DEFENCES, AND THE EMERGENCE OF EGO PSYCHOLOGY: HARTMANN, MAHLER, SPITZ, ERIKSON, AND KOHUT

Anna Freud was both a devoted daughter and a devoted Freudian, but often her contribution in further exploring the ego has been underestimated. Apart from being a pioneer in child psychoanalysis, she also reshaped the role and focus of the analyst in the therapeutic process by pointing out the gap in both the *topographical* and the *structural* models in dealing with the patient's defence mechanisms. More specifically she postulated that a proper analytic attitude should be 'neutral' and pay even attention to all three parts of the mind (i.e. id, ego, and superego) that co-create the neurotic structures. If the analyst's attention is concentrated on the patient's free associations as a means of accessing the id content, then how can the patient break through the defences that will inevitably hold back their free associations at some point? The ego's unconscious defence constructs cannot be underestimated and therefore need to be facilitated to the surface.

Her seminal book *Ego and the Mechanisms of Defence* is one of the clearest descriptions of Sigmund Freud's 12 defence mechanisms (i.e. *introjection, identification, turning against the self, reversal, sublimation/displacement, denial, repression, regression, reaction-formation, isolation of affect, undoing, projection*). Anna Freud added also two defences that presented issues of women and of minorities, as we could see now from a more political view: an *act of altruism* and *identification with the aggressor* (the latter was first coined by Ferenczi, but Anna Freud omitted referring to his work).

Anna Freud's approach is characterised by a more egalitarian attitude from the analyst to the patient and by a much more considerate attitude to the patient's ego and superego. She saw the child psychoanalyst as a figure who needs to gain their child-patient's trust with some *preparatory period* so that the first becomes an ally to the latter (see also later on the term *therapeutic alliance*), and they support them in having some sense of their disturbance; especially considering that children don't usually choose themselves to enter analysis. The analyst is also an educator, given the children's undeveloped superego and their need for someone to give them the sense of right and wrong. Anna Freud advocated that these are ideas applicable also to teachers, childcare providers, adopting carers, etc.

She saw adolescence as the period of the ego's main struggle for survival and for taming the instinctual forces that upsurge during this developmental stage. This means that all methods of defence are on the surface too.

Anna Freud developed a form of creating a whole picture of a child's development called *developmental lines*. This was her attempt to tackle the reliance on isolated facts and to highlight the normal development of a child alongside their psychopathology. Her language of *fixations and developmental arrests* is now used by several disciplines and her belief in the healthy parts of a child in addition to the *developmental lines* have been the fundamentals for the 'Kestenberg Movement Profile', a movement observation and treatment tool developed by the child psychoanalyst Judith Kestenberg.

She also brought back the focus on the external factors and realities that create feelings associated with threat (e.g. abuse, neglect); therefore, defences in her work were either against instincts or against affects.

HEINZ HARTMANN AND EGO PSYCHOLOGY IN THE USA

Hartmann, the founder of *ego psychology*, took further Anna Freud's ideas on the normal and adaptive aspects of the patients' personality, as well as her re-emphasis on the vital connection between the ego and the external world.

He did some deeper questioning of the original Freudian theory on conflict and moved beyond the idea of the personality as a battlefield. For Hartmann the non-defensive and adaptive parts of the ego can create *conflict-free spheres*, thus the ego being able to interact with the external world free from internal influences. All this depends, of course, on how favourable the environmental influences are, bringing again attention to the shaping influence of the environment on the development of personality. That conflict-free part of the ego includes the thinking, learning, and languageing functions, as well as memory and rational planning.

Hartmann's theory was also a step further away from concentrating on repressed primitive impulses and he emphasised the reparations of certain dimensions in the psyche, introducing in this way the importance of *adaptation*.

MARGARET MAHLER AND RENÉ SPITZ: DEVELOPMENTAL EGO PSYCHOLOGY

Mahler and Spitz are perceived as the *developmental ego psychologists* whose methodological way (see systematic studies of controlled infant observation) of theory production took child psychoanalysis to another level in terms of normal and abnormal development, making the environment a vital factor.

Spitz's work left a legacy in the change of the caring system in the USA with two terms he coined in relation to emotional deprivation: *anaclitic depression* (partial emotional deprivation) and *hospitalism* (total deprivation). His main thesis was that no matter how much inborn psychological potential an infant has, they will not be able to reach that if there is no emotional connectedness with another human in their environment. He also paid attention to the *libidinal object* and their importance in providing an infant with that essential human connectedness that facilitates psychological development, but that object is not to be taken for granted as they are a developmental achievement.

Spitz shifted the focus on early life by describing the infant as both *undifferentiated* (how the infant's individual psyche is) and *nondifferentiated* (see the infant alone to 'infant-with-mother'). This means that the infant is in great need of a gradual acquisition of the capacity to function independently and any kind of deprivation or neglect can have irreparable results.

Another important contribution by Spitz was his highlighting of the use of touch, senses, movement, and rhythm in the contact between the mother and her infant, creating in this way a total *sensing system* that accommodates the infant's *reception* – rather than perception – of expressive signals. This is one of the first points in psychoanalysis where there is a mind–body continuum and where the field between the mother and her infant is described as reciprocal and co-influencing, highlighting in this way the concept of adaptation in ego psychology and the psychic plasticity that this gives.

Mahler's work was concentrated on children with psychosis (whether living with their families or in hospitals), which was by itself radical given the more selective attitude to psychopathology within the psychoanalytic tradition.

Continuing Spitz's highlighting of the importance of early relationships, Mahler developed her theory around the sense of identity and formation of the self. She saw these developing out of a crucial early merger experience with the mother. If that fails or if there is no resolution to the disruption of this process, then we are talking about certain kinds of disturbance and a confusion of who the infant (or patient) is. In other words, Mahler sees environmental factors (i.e. traumatic experiences or the mother not being able to provide the 'safe anchorage' for the infant to explore their symbiotic experience) as the main reason for any kind of disturbance, instead of what Anna Freud and Mahler's predecessors would see as a problem in the direction of the infant's libidinal energy.

For Mahler the toddler starts exploring the constancy of the mother at around seven months old and this is a crucial time for their development: they apply their curiosity to the world and start going off, but they always need to come back to their mother for reassurance that she is there and that she has not abandoned them. This is the starting point for *separation-individuation* which ideally leads to the child's capacity to retain a mental image or memory of the absent or not immediately accessed mother.

The analytic relationship and experience can be a corrective symbiotic experience, with the analyst's absence during breaks or on weekends being the test for the separation–individuation process.

OFFSHOOTS OF EGO PSYCHOLOGY: ERIKSON AND KOHUT TOWARDS A MORE INCLUSIVE DEFINITION OF IDENTITY AND THE SELF

Erik Erikson with his *psychosocial development theory* and Heinz Kohut with his *self psychology* theory took further the psychoanalytic vision of ego psychology by recognising and highlighting the complexity and depth of subjectivity beyond the realm of instinctual conflict and more in connection with the individual's cultural and social context.

These two theories can be seen as complementary innovations in elaborating on the concept of identity (Erikson) and developing the notion of the self (Kohut).

Erikson's work became very famous outside the psychoanalytic tradition as he added the psychosocial dimension to the Freudian psychobiological one as equal components for personality development; culture and history were for him equally important roots for development. He showed the interpenetrability of individual and culture by creating a framework, where the core of the individual and the core of their communal culture are in a complex dialectical relationship, where the psychological interacts and affects the social and vice versa. Therefore, identity formation is a kind of *psychosocial relativity*.

In Erikson's theory, where the individual is placed in their historical time and cultural context, the mother is seen as the representative and main means of introducing the infant to the certain culture they were born; she organises and evaluates the basic needs of safety, pleasure, and gratification – alongside their opposites – that then shape the infant's experiences and identity.

Ego development, in Erikson's terms, is not a step-by-step process across the life cycle but more of a complex and gradually unfolding set of vital tensions that are in constant resonance too. His work on adolescence is an example of this: adolescence is a transition from childhood to adulthood and, consequently, the beginning of the intersection between the individual and the social world with all its multilayered tensions that culture and history bring.

Kohut's self psychology theory explored the phenomenology of selfhood, placing the individual in the centre of a struggle for meaning-making, for soothing of their isolation. His fresh view was based on the emergence of a deep and complex personal subjectivity within an interpersonal and cultural context. His view of the patient was that of a 'tragic' figure, rather than a guilty one, over their forbidden wishes. Kohut believed that flourishing happens in certain kinds of environments that facilitate the child to grow up with a deep sense of feeling human, not just being one. His work reveals his deep respect for and appreciation of the patient's often ill-fated but ever hopeful attempts to keep growing despite adversity.

Kohut's psychoanalytic stance came to address a significant gap in psychoanalytic theory: the importance of empathy in the therapeutic relationship. He pinpointed the beginning of the need for empathy from the infant's narcissistic phase, which he saw as a totally normal part of development. Considering the infant as a whole self who seeks relationships from the beginning of their life, we can see why the caregiver needs to initially respond to the infant with an attitude of gratifying the infant's wish for admiration (*mirroring*), as well as idealisation and unity (*twinship*). Even though this is not a state that can persist in later child development, introducing frustration needs to be gradual and sensitive to the child's needs. In this sense, the key attitude of the caregiver needs to be one of empathy and attunement. Kohut saw pathological narcissism as a result of trauma and failure of empathy and perceived the therapeutic relationship as parallel to the relationship between an infant and their caregiver. Therefore, he postulated that the analyst needs to maintain a consistent empathic stance towards their patient's subjective reality, in an attempt to heal any narcissistic injuries. Lack of empathy by the analyst can result in shame.

Kohut's other important innovation was the use of the term *self-object* to describe the early relationship between the child and the mother as well as the therapeutic relationship. Self-object is neither self nor other; it is the assimilation of the other within oneself, which is not seen though as pathological but as a way to maintain the self with security and interest.

To develop a healthy self, the infant needs to experience the mother as part of oneself which can be unconditionally available. As the child matures, self-object relationships are replaced by object relations and an internalised *nurturing self-object*, with the understanding that the individual has received some *empathic mirroring* from the nurturing parent, and later on from their analyst.

MELANIE KLEIN AND OBJECT RELATIONS THEORIES: BION, FAIRBAIRN, WINNICOTT, AND BOWLBY

MELANIE KLEIN AND THE BEGINNINGS OF THE OBJECT RELATIONS SCHOOL

Melanie Klein's theory had an equally big impact to Freud's within psychoanalytic circles and her legacy affected both the *object relations school* as well as Jungian and even humanistic trainings. In her work we can see the beginnings of the object relations school and the overall turn towards relatedness as the essence of human nature. Hers is a theory that searched the meaning of pain in life rather than its joys, and this is palpable throughout when the emphasis is on anxiety rather than well-being.

Differences from Freud

Klein always defended her theories as directly stemming from Freud's ones and that she continued his work rather than differentiating herself from what he originally said. Indeed, she initially extended Freud's theory to earlier developmental stages, highlighting in this way the early impact of the Oedipus complex and of the terrifying superego with its ferocious early form of conscience. According to Klein both those elements are present in an infant's life from early on and take the form of primitive terrors. Nevertheless, Klein's focus was very different from Freud's one and the two theorists' distinctive differences can be summarised as follows:

- Freud's description of the instinct in relation to libidinal energy was that of an impulse that has a source (see erogenous zones), an aim (see discharge), and an object. His theory emphasised the first two only, so Klein emphasised the latter and particularly the anxieties about and for the things and people which the child relates to.
- Klein's view on early development was focused on how anxiety is experienced and managed by the infant, unlike Freud's focus on the experience of sexuality from infancy on.
- Klein's image of the ego at early developmental stages is a discontinuous one governed by phantasies and terrors, whilst for Freud it is the cohesive and integrated ego that deals with the libidinal and aggressive impulses of early life.
- The most important difference, though, is Klein's challenge of Freud's self-gratifying individual who needs to be introduced to relationships. Klein saw the individual as conditioned to be emotionally interdependent from the beginning of their life. Therefore, she saw personality development and formation as the outcome of the continuous interpersonal journey between

the individual and their primary objects, and the psyche as always unstable due to its fight back of anxieties.

Here I would like to clarify the difference between **ph**antasy and **f**antasy, the first being a fundamental concept in Klein's theory. Fantasy represents the imaginative fulfilment of suppressed conscious/unconscious desires, whilst the Kleinian phantasy describes the infant's state of mind during the early stages of development, and it acts as a bridge between instinct and thought.

Klein's view of the infant–caregiver relationship and the two positions

Klein's theories placed much emphasis on the mother–child dyad, and she insisted that this relationship starts from birth and impacts the development of the human psyche. The Kleinian infant is an active emotional and relational being who reaches out to the mother, even though initially they see her as a fragmented person, rather than as a complete one. The infant's emotional reactions shape their overall development, and their subjective agency in the world supports the continuous demands for relationships, as well as the anxieties, conflicts, and changes that affect life.

The infant's inner world is characterised by both hatred and love. Klein used the terms *envy* and *gratitude*; the first describing the urge to spoil what is good due to its existence outside the self (see e.g. the envied mother's breast which can meet the baby's hunger-need but is outside the baby's self) and the second describing that essential part in the infant's relation to the mother from the beginning of their life together. These two feelings represent the death and life instincts, with Klein paying much attention to the first and its leading to feelings of destructive rage.

Klein talked of *positions* rather than developmental stages, and the two positions I will describe next are seen in constant oscillation throughout life as the individual tries to protect themselves from their destructive states of mind. They are also seen as constellations of phantasies, anxieties, and defences with their main aim being the protection of the individual from their own internal destructiveness.

The *paranoid-schizoid position* predominates in the baby's first three months and it's their way to manage and make sense of the chaos they experience with the interplay between anxieties and deprivations–disruptions after birth and in their early post-natal life. The anxieties are about the self and its survival and well-being. The infant tries to organise their anxious experiences of disintegration and annihilation by *splitting* them into good or bad and/or *projecting* them.

Splitting is an early defence mechanism where the infant sharply divides the object (e.g. the mother or her breast) into good and bad parts, and thus, the object no longer has integrity and a whole structure. To protect the good experience, the baby *splits off* and *projects* any bad experiences (e.g. hunger) into the *bad object* that is mainly felt as dangerous and persecutory. The good experiences are then projected into the *good object* that is idealised. The emotional attitude towards the split objects is antithetical. The *good* and *bad breast* are the classical part-objects on which the baby focuses initially. The term includes both the actual breast as well as the mother in her solely feeding role. Similarly, she believed that the intra-psychic representations of aspects of relations with significant others (*internal objects*) are experienced by the infant – and later by the adult – as either good or bad, depending on the experience of the external object.

During the process of *projection* there can also be the process of *projective identification* where the mother identifies with the denied feelings or experiences that have been projected into her from her infant. This process has a strong element of relief for the infant as they get rid of painful and unbearable parts of themselves that give them anxiety, and they might also build up an illusion of having control over their mother.

In the second half of the baby's first year there is the developmental achievement of realising that the hated object is also the one that satisfies their instincts and is loved. This achievement results in ambivalence and guilt, and this is when the baby enters the *depressive position*. Here the anxiety is not so much about the survival of the self but, mainly, the survival of the object upon whom the baby depends. The feeling of anger towards the punitive and hated object is now replaced by grief when the baby experiences the absence of the desired good; the baby is no longer deprived or punished but they feel the loss. Depression is seen as the baby's reaction after the transformation of the outward anger against the bad object into an inward kind of anger against themselves. And this transformation is the result of the baby's fear of their own anger and a desperate attempt to not destroy the object that is now perceived and experienced as one (bad and good together).

How have you experienced love and hatred at the same time in important relationships in your life?

Where did ambivalence, guilt, anger, and grief stand during those splitting moments in your life?

Finally, Klein postulated that one's superego is also formed very early in their lives through the experience of taking in the emotional experience of the parental figures (*introjection*). The introjected parental figures can be analysed into a number of components, the *introjects* – that is the good/bad internal mother/father.

Kleinian psychoanalytic work with children

One of Klein's most important innovations was her framework and play techniques for working with children which was structured around her desire to hear the story that was hidden inside each child's emotional life. She developed her work with the main idea of free play taking the place of free associations; thus she worked with children who had some verbal communication – from around the age of 2 and a half and onwards.

The set-up of individual drawers with the content of small, simple, non-mechanical toys represented the inner world of the child that was then shared with their analyst. The nature of the toys allowed for some imaginative rather than technical play, and the small human figures pointed towards the relationships with and between objects. The toys were the objects in the child's active mind and showed their unconscious phantasies.

Klein's theory applied into therapy

In Kleinian therapy there is the image of a *total transference* situation in which everything that is said and done is explored under the lens of transference towards the analyst and with unconscious meaning. There is a strong relational dimension as the patient is seen having the potential to have a focus on making reparations and reconstituting the long lost or damaged good object that exists in their minds.

Projective identification is of great value in this approach as it forms a major part of the countertransference. As the patient projects disavowed and/or unbearable aspects of themselves into the analyst, the latter becomes unconsciously identified with them and may behave or feel accordingly. The analyst passes the threshold of projective identification and moves towards countertransference when they start being more aware of this unconscious process.

Bion's main contributions to psychoanalysis were his work with groups and patients with schizophrenia, his notion of the *container* and *contained*, and his pioneering use of ignorance and 'not knowing' in the therapeutic relationship.

He was critical about the psychoanalytic tendency to suggest that everything belongs to the past and that everything is explained in transference terms, and he introduced the term *negative capability* for the analyst's desire for their patient's progress and also their memories of what they think they know about their patients – based on the latter's history and on material from previous sessions. Bion saw these as obstacles in the 'there and then', in the moment, and in a way, he brought back onto the surface of clinical thinking Freud's intention for the analysts to function with receptivity and listening without expectations. He believed that psychoanalysis was not only about getting to know one's self but mainly getting to being one's own self through a journey of transformations.

Working with patients with schizophrenia was an inspiration for Bion to take Klein's notion of envy a step further. For Bion the fragmentation experienced by his patients was a demonstration of their envious attacks not only on the object but also on the part of the person's (or child's) mind that is/was connected to the object and reality, a self-attack that eventually breaks all connections among people, feelings, thoughts, and facts. This attack on linking creates those fragments that resulted in Bion considering what the analyst does with them, when experiencing projective identification in an interpersonalised way in the therapeutic relationship. Thus, he talked about the analyst (and the mother) as a container of all that material that the patient (and the child) cannot contain and needs to discharge via projective identification. The analyst from their side is affected by this emotional exchange, but they use their organisational capacities to translate those projections into some sort of meaningful, integrated, and digestible thoughts for the patient. In this way the client (and originally the infant) makes sense of their experience and takes in an object that can bear their anxiety, which is not destroyed or which will not abandon them. In other words, Bion believed in a positive form of projective identification that is underlined by empathy and in which the analyst/mother contains the painful and hostile projections, *detoxifies* them, and then returns them to the patient/infant in a more digestible form and at the right moment.

Bion's work with groups was very much focused on their intra-tensions and the assumed functions of *dependency* on the leader, *fight against/flight from* an external threat, and *pairing* of phantasies or even *pairing* of two members and expulsion, to gain some hope and protect themselves from despair.

OBJECT RELATIONS THEORIES AND THE 'INDEPENDENTS' OR MIDDLE GROUP

The British Psychoanalytical Society (BPS) suffered from many splits after the Freud family arrived in the UK and Anna Freud and the Freudians entered a long-term conflict with the Kleinians. The cumulation of those conflicts were the 'controversial discussions', a series of talks with acrimonious debates in the early '40s. After that the BPS split into three groups: the Freudians, the Kleinians, and the 'independents' or middle group. We have seen so far the theories of Sigmund and Anna Freud, as well as those of Melanie Klein and her direct follower, Wilfred Bion.

The independent group developed non-Kleinian versions of what is now known as *object relations theories*. Based on Klein's perception of the infant as wired for human interaction and on relationships being the foundation for the sense of being human, this group of theorists deviated from Klein's principle of built-in aggression that stems from the death instinct. Their view of the infant is one born to harmoniously interact with their environment but whose development can be ruptured, or traumatised, by inadequate parenting. The human being was seen as dependent on relationships, rather than as a system of biological drives. Their work highlighted the importance of nurturance of childhood for the development of healthy societies and, therefore, some of them made a big contribution to social care and health policies (e.g. Donald Winnicott and John Bowlby).

When seen as a school of thought, object relations consists of diverse perspectives based on the premise that the need for relationship is primary and that this is what makes the self a composite of internal relationships – at both conscious and unconscious levels. Next I will describe the works of Ronald Fairbairn, Winnicott, and Bowlby, but I would also like to mention and signpost you to the works of Harry Guntrip and Sylvia Payne, Marjorie Brierley, Ella Freeman Sharpe, Paula Heimann, Michael and Enid Balint, John Rickman, Masud Khan, and Michael Foulkes.

RONALD FAIRBAIRN: TOWARDS A DYNAMIC STRUCTURE OF THE SELF

Fairbairn's contribution to psychoanalysis is innovative and revolutionary. He created an object relations theory of personality that considered inadequate parenting and environmental factors for the understanding of internal objects. For him biology didn't make sense as he saw the whole human organism as an entity formed in relationships, and this is where we can see the more established elements of a relational view of psychoanalysis.

Fairbairn saw the infant as a realist who, from the very beginning of their life, seeks relationship with their caregivers. The infant's focus is not pleasure but attachment and relationship, as if relationships are the pleasure. He defines pleasure as a wonderful connector with the caregivers, so when the latter engage in pleasurable exchanges with the infant, they give them a learning experience for their connections and interactions. Fairbairn's infant, as we can see, is wired for interaction, and their ego, which is present from birth, is the only player in the structural model of the mind. He also saw libido as a function of the ego and aggression as an organising factor for frustrations and deprivation.

An important deviation from Klein's object relations theory is that Fairbairn's internal objects represent substitutes that compensate for the real thing, actual people in the world of relationships when there is no healthy parenting, when the infant's needs are not met, and therefore, the infant makes a pathological turning away from external reality.

Infantile stages of development and states

Given Fairbairn's non-acceptance of biology, it is not surprising that he reformulated Freud's stages of development. For him any developmental stages had to do with the infant's ability to form relationships with the object(s) at different stages after birth.

(1) *Infantile dependence*: this is the stage of total and inescapable dependence. The mother's breast is a natural biological object and the infant's mouth relates to it.
   • Early oral stage: sucking or rejecting (see *schizoid state* next)
   • Late oral stage: sucking or biting (*ambivalence*)
(2) *Quasi independence*: here the internal objects are divided into good and bad, and they are gradually externalised. It's a transitional stage from infantile dependence to mature dependence.
(3) *Mature dependence*: this is the stage of full self-object differentiation and of mutual relationships with whole objects. Both accepted and rejected objects have been exteriorised by now, and it's a stage that reflects the individual's giving attitude.

Following Klein's theorising of different positions as responses to the bad object, Fairbairn also sees the infant dealing with their fundamental trauma of maternal indifference with either a schizoid response (by imagining that their love has destroyed their mother's feelings) or a depressive one (by imagining that their hate has annihilated them as a dyad – corresponding to the late oral stage and the ambivalence that dominates that stage). Given that everyone's childhood has some sort of pain or trauma, these two states are part of everyone's experience.

Fairbairn also saw repression as part of this relational web, with its failures and fears. What he believed, though, is that the *repressed* is actual relationships and ties to certain qualities of the caregivers that cannot be integrated into other relational structures. He defined the *repressed* as that part of the self who is tied to inaccessible – and often dangerous – features of the caregivers, and the *repressor* as that part of the self who is tied to more accessible – and less dangerous – features of the caregivers. Both parts are internal relationships.

Splitting of the ego and internal objects

In Fairbairn's theory splitting is a regulating defence mechanism that dissects and organises the ego (self) and is the result of abuse, deprivation, or neglect. Given his view that everyone has had less than ideal parenting, we can understand why he presumed splitting of the ego is a universal phenomenon.

When a caregiver is emotionally unavailable (e.g. depression or violent attitude), the child becomes connected with and absorbs the only available qualities by the parents, the unresponsive ones. This internalisation of the relationship with the caregiver(s) creates a split in the ego:

- Part of the self maintains their direction and response-seeking towards the real caregiver in the external world
- Part of the self deviates their direction towards the illusory caregivers as internal objects

This first split and internalisation are followed by another split:

- The *exciting/libidinal object* represents the caregiver's promising and captivating qualities
- The *rejecting/antilibidinal object* represents the frustrating and disappointing qualities

As the ego is in need of a good relationship with the caregiver(s), for the infant to survive, another split of the ego takes place. In that later split the resulting internal situation is of the original ego containing the *central (conscious) ego/I* – the remainder of the undivided self which is attached to the *ideal object* – as well as the *repressed libidinal ego*, which is attached to the *exciting object*, and the *repressed antilibidinal ego*, which is attached to the *rejecting object*.

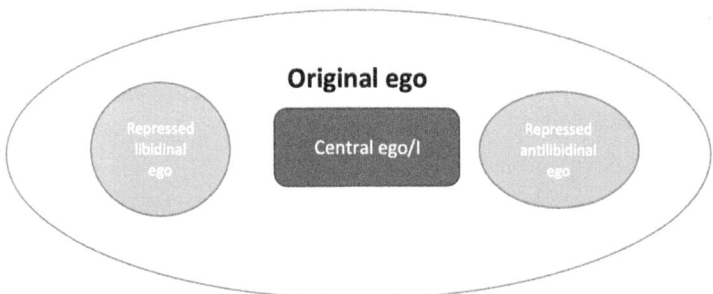

Fairbairn's ego model

This is a cyclical sequence of internal processes as one goes through life and relationships with important others. Thus, Fairbairn postulated, there is repetition of relational patterns where each of us projects their internal object relations onto new interpersonal situations.

Understandably, then, we can see why it is difficult to break through such deeply rooted patterns and disturbances.

Psychic growth and analytic change

For Fairbairn psychic growth comes with great acceptance of oneself, as well as with greater acceptance of others. When the client sees themselves as good enough, rather than as idealised or denigrated, and when they use this lens for their relationship with other – that is no projections but accepting attitude – then they start the process of re-externalising the internal objects which had become splits and, therefore, opening up to the possibility of new relationships with good objects.

Maturation is also seen as a movement from immature to mature dependency, but dependency is always integral to living in this world. Fairbairn criticised the idealisation of autonomy in the Western world as a false goal, imposed by consumerist societies.

In the analytic situation what becomes the focus is the actual relationship with the analyst, rather than any interpretations or transferential processes. A congruent relationship with the analyst who shows that they see the client in their fullness can allow the latter to let go of their attachments to their internal objects and to gain an ability to connect with the former in new ways (*analytic change*).

Fairbairn introduced some modifications to the analytic setting to tackle the repetition of dynamics that led to his clients' traumas of abandonment and deprivation. More specifically, he gave his patients the option to sit in a chair, half-facing him, and he would sit behind a desk.

DONALD WINNICOTT: IN SEARCH OF THE GOOD ENOUGH MOTHER

Winnicott's theory and work were characterised by innovation, creativity, and optimism as he tried to reconcile drive theory with the interpersonal perspective, as a consequence of the shift of the middle group towards a more intersubjective understanding of human development. He tried to understand the mutual interplay between internal and external objects, as opposed to their separate view. For this process he coined the term *potential space* that describes the experience of that mutual interplay as neither inside nor outside, but in between. As a paediatrician he based his theories on thousands of hours of direct observations of mothers and babies.

A radical aspect of Winnicott's work was his view of psychoanalysis as a process of learning to play. If playing is the equivalent of free association, then any material that needed to be aired would emerge through play organically; with adults, play would be more about *talking nonsense*. His way of working was non-intrusive, and he saw the analyst as a *holding* presence rather than the authority that uses interpretations to achieve self-revelation.

As he deviated from the original child analytic thinking of both Klein and Freud, he developed respect for the need to be *hidden* and therefore placed much less importance on the aims of uncovering the unconscious, of revealing the aggression; for Winnicott interaction, holding, and a sense of love modelling were primary aims and qualities for any analytic relationship. For his principle of encouraging interaction he invented the *squiggle game*, a form of symbolisation of unresolved conflicts where analyst and child-patient take turns in creating shapes like doodles that can turn into something more concrete.

The baby

Unlike the founder of object relations theory and his supervisor, Melanie Klein, he saw the baby as unintentionally destructive due to its love for the caregiver. For Winnicott the symptoms a baby was demonstrating were a sign of health as they were trying to come into a place of equilibrium. He also placed special emphasis on the external environment and the impact on the baby. Given that he developed his theory after the Second World War and with traumatised children, it is not surprising that he included the context in both his theory and his practice (see later on his view of the analytic situation). Winnicott saw humans as absolutely sociable, and similarly, he believed that there is no such thing as a baby on their own. Any individual is in an ongoing process of emerging from a matrix of communality since their birth.

The mother

For Winnicott the mother is pre-occupied with and projects onto the baby way before the latter is born. This maternal state of mind (*primary maternal pre-occupation*) lasts several weeks after birth and shows the mother's capacity for acute tuning in as she becomes withdrawn from her own subjectivity, ignores the external world, and creates for the baby and herself a form of illusionary oneness where she 'brings the world' to her baby. This process fosters the *subjective omnipotence* necessary for the baby's development, in which they believe that their own wish creates the object of desire.

A *good enough* mother is one who meets her baby's symbiotic needs, follows her baby's timing, and provides consistent empathy and *holding*. The latter is a concept Winnicott developed in relation to the *environmental mother* who organises and maintains a physical and psychical space within which her baby is protected without them knowing so. Holding is not offered on an ongoing basis as it is equally vital that the mother knows when she is not needed.

As the good enough experience of the dyad mother–baby unfolds, the mother gradually starts to reclaim her own mind–body state whilst she opens up the space for her child's movement away from the original nest.

Another vital role that Winnicottian mothers play for their babies is that of mirroring their babies' feelings through their facial and embodied expressions. The mother's visual responsiveness allows the baby to build up their sense of self and to develop some healthy narcissism.

Finally, Winnicott recognised that mothers can feel both love and hatred towards their babies; the point, though, is how much and for how long these contradictory feelings last.

Transitional space and experience

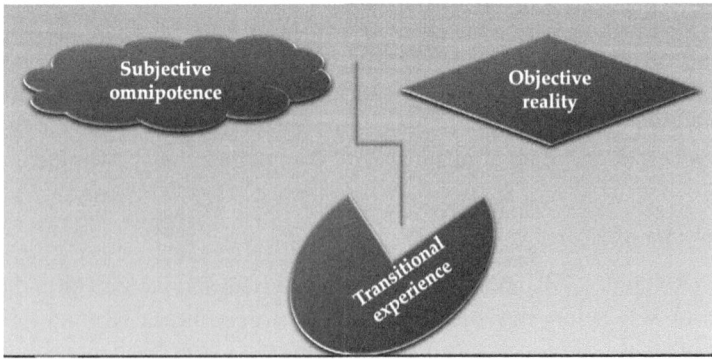

Winnicott's transitional process

The transitional space is a place of creativity in which the child plays (or the adult talks) and where inner and outer life contribute. The adjective 'transitional' indicates that the mode of experience organising is neither subjective nor objective, neither inner nor outer; in other words, it's a place that is neither self nor other. There are two scenarios where this fluidity (*transitional process*) between the forming self and the shifting reality is not balanced:

First, we can consider a person who lived primarily within their *subjective omnipotence* and never built a bridge with the *objective reality*; they tend to be self-absorbed and in their own mind–body bubble. The second scenario is when a person has no roots in their subjective omnipotence and therefore functions purely from the base of the objective reality; they then tend to be superficially adjusted and lacking passion and originality.

In this transitional space the baby needs some 'not me' objects to use in the process of separation from the primary love object (*transitional object*). These are objects that provide soothing and autonomy when the comforting mother is not around and are usually with a characteristic odor and feeling (e.g. teddy bears, blankies, scarves). Equally, *transitional phenomena* include sounds (e.g. singing for sleep) or material objects that are not fully recognised as parts of the external reality and which counteract feelings of object loss or abandonment.

True vs. false self

When the good enough mother facilitates the subjective omnipotence of her child, she also facilitates the formation of a creative and playful self. This is the *true self* who needs a well-established omnipotence before the reality, with its pain and losses, is introduced into the child's mind–body awareness and the child is able to face the consequence of the pain and losses. If the mother is not good enough, then we can see how the child forms a compliant *false self*, where the child adapts to the others' needs rather than expressing their own needs (see situations of emotional or other deprivation and of violent impingements on early experiences).

In extreme cases of unresponsiveness from the mother, the baby – and then the adult – could develop a *false self disorder*, a form of psychopathology where the quality of personhood – one's subjectivity – is disordered.

Do you remember your first transitional object and how did you part from it?
Have you considered who has been a 'holding' figure in your life?
How often do you notice yourself or others using the terms 'true and false self' in everyday conversations?

Theory in action

Winnicott's approach was characterised by empathy and a thoughtful and inclusive attitude towards both his child and adult patients. His was an analytic situation that inspired emotional closeness, a more relaxed sense of boundaries, and a playful attunement to patients. The analyst's holding is seen as essential in the process of reintroduction of neglected or pushed away self structures, so that the true self can emerge. The analyst is at the disposal of the self-healing patient and what they need to reclaim as a missed experience.

JOHN BOWLBY AND THE PRIMACY OF THE NEED FOR RELATIONSHIP

Bowlby's work is perceived to have had the deepest impact on social policies in terms of preventative work as well as strategies on separation of babies from parents (see e.g. premature babies). He is also well-known for his research-oriented psychoanalytic theories and practice and for bridging his discipline with ethology (observation of animals), cybernetics (feedback systems or information processing), anthropology, biology, and other sciences.

Attachment theory is based on the premise that relationships and the relational structure of the self are essential for the development of an individual. Survival is dependent on relationships and bonds. It is a theory that endeavoured also to provide objective evidence for object relations theories.

Attachment is defined as the child's tie to the mother, and Bowlby postulated that that is instinctual and not acquired and is similar to the bonding processes seen in other mammals. Therefore, it is a primary function rather than a derivative of the mother's need-gratifying interventions in the baby's development. Dependency, in other words, is seen as integral to the human condition, as opposed to the societal tendencies for autonomy that stem from a false conception of human relationships within the context of consumerist societies.

The modes of relating and exploring we all learn from experience contribute to an *internal working model* of the world. This is our internal base which includes emotional, behavioural, and cognitive representations of self, other, and their in-between relationship.

Any temporary or permanent separation from the primary attachment figures (*secure base*), whose presence is felt to be essential to survival, can cause a crisis demonstrated in *separation anxiety*. Some examples of this anxiety are clinging or fearful behaviours that, if they are prolonged, culminate in a *mourning process*. The world cannot be explored without the existence of this secure base which gives the sense of refuge for the baby to embark on exploration but also know that they can return.

The ultimate aim of the baby's attachment to the mother (or caregiver) is the necessary proximity with them to receive protection from danger and affect regulation, especially for the unbearable feelings of fear and distress. Attachment patterns and styles start at the age of 6 months and they develop as the internal working model is also built up through maternal responsiveness. The baby gradually gains a sense of agency as they take in the interaction between internal and external worlds.

In this theory, too, we can see the crucial role of the mother in the child's early development and the emphasis on maternal ability in direct connection with emotional stability. For Bowlby it was *maternal deprivation* that caused neurosis and relational problems in adulthood. He also postulated that defences stem from the process of detachment as this is seen when the fundamental need for attachment is deactivated.

Attachment styles

Bowlby's co-researcher and colleague at the Tavistock Clinic, Mary Ainsworth, conducted the pieces of research on which Bowlby based his classification of attachment styles. Ainsworth developed the *strange situation* observational model to test a baby's attachment quality towards their mother. The mother was perceived as the *secure base* from which the baby would confidently be able to explore the world. The spatial proximity allowed for a controllable level of anxiety.

The mother's role is to encourage and model the development of a balanced and reciprocal relationship that would inspire a *secure attachment*. An over-anxious reaction to the baby's explorations has the potential of inhibited explorations and suffocation for the baby (*anxious-ambivalent attachment*), whilst a neglectful response might cause dangerous explorations and, in the end, some overwhelming anxiety (*avoidant-dismissive attachment*). A fourth classification was identified and theoretically developed in the '80s. A *disorganised-disoriented attachment* happens in a caregiving situation with unresolved loss when the baby's internal working model is flooded with fear, anger, or other unbearable feelings and they employ desperate strategies in their interactions with the primary caregiver.

Attachment theory in action

Attachment psychotherapy emphasises the intersubjective nature of the therapeutic relationship, where early experiences of attachment can be relived and processed through re-enactments with the therapist. The therapist also embodies the presence that is – and was – needed for the client's development of a secure attachment.

THE NEO-FREUDIANS OR CULTURALISTS: SULLIVAN, HORNEY, AND FROMM

HARRY STACK SULLIVAN AND INTERPERSONAL PSYCHIATRY

Sullivan's interpersonal theory placed special emphasis on relatedness and the here and now and saw the analyst as an active inquirer into their patients' interactions, marking a significant contrast with the classical psychoanalytic model.

Working with patients with schizophrenia made Sullivan curious and sensitive in understanding and making meaning of interactions that have had such an impact on his patients that they developed psychopathology. For him psychopathology could no longer be explained on an individual basis; humans are inseparable from their interpersonal field. Therefore, Sullivan developed his theory around the importance of studying the interpersonal field rather than the individual (the self not inside the individual but in interaction with others). To look at the patient's interpersonal field and history the analyst needs to look at both their past and their present relationships and interactions. Internal tensions are no longer seen as the result of repressed wishes and fantasies but of unattended interactions.

Fear and anxiety are distinguishable, and Sullivan saw the latter as the cause of psychopathology. A newborn experiences an oscillating state between comfort and tension. The caregiver's role is to respond reasonably to these tensions. The infant's needs require complementarity and that's why Sullivan called them *integrating tendencies*; the needs draw people together in a mutually satisfying integration. Fear arises when there are tensions and unfulfilled needs, but its expression brings the caregiver into an interaction with the infant, with the aim of soothing them.

On the other hand, Sullivan saw anxiety as an outwardly induced feeling: as infants are particularly sensitive to their caregivers' feeling states, the latter's feelings are contagious (*empathic linkage*). Because the source of rescuing from the destabilising feelings is also the source of anxiety, the infant experiences a formless tension with no focus and escape route. A sense of disintegration can develop, which Sullivan also saw in adults suffering from anxiety, and then being unable to satisfy their needs.

The infant (and child and adult) then creates clusters of nonanxious states called *good mother* and of anxious states called *bad mother*. These are not only in connection with the mother but also to any caregiver in the infant's life. Gradually the infant shifts from a passive experience of these states to a more dynamic one where they can predict which of the two 'mothers' (i.e. experiences) is approaching. The infant also starts discovering that whichever 'mother' appears has something to do with them. So, the next level of clustering involves the infant's activities that generate approval and therefore soothing for them (*good me*), those that generate anxiety and therefore an anxious state for them (*bad me*), and finally, those activities that generate intense anxiety and are not experienced as parts of them (*not me*) that result in dissociation.

In his theory of personality, Sullivan highlighted the intense connection and reliance of the formation of the self-system on the personalities of the important others, and consequently the inner tensions and psychopathologies this process can cause. For him, though, the self-system might be conservative, but it is not fixed, which then allows for reparative experiences in analysis.

Sullivan saw the analyst's engagement with the analytic process and their patients' material as *participant observation*, thus, his approach being characterised by active participation, detailed enquiry, and person-to-person qualities. He is also remembered as the first psychoanalyst who identified as a gay man and tried to prevent homosexuality from being pathologised.

KAREN HORNEY AND ERICH FROMM: THE INTERPERSONALISTS/ CULTURALISTS

Karen Horney and Erich Fromm influenced each other's work and thinking about human development and they both borrowed elements from Adler's theory. They belong to the interpersonalists/culturalists alongside Sullivan as they highlighted the importance of relationships and socio-political structures for actualisation and contributed in reviewing the analytic relationship as one of adult-to-adult rather than a parent–child dynamic.

Horney's review of Freud's theory of personality cost her her membership in the American psychoanalytic community but also paved the way for the later feminist view on psychoanalysis and the refusal to just follow what all the male figures had been preaching regarding neuroses and female sexuality.

Her theory combined the Adlerian focus on social factors, with Sullivan's interpersonal stance and a more optimistic view of human nature. Horney saw pathological behaviour as a result of the blocked or oppressed innate forces for reaching one's potential by external social forces. Her opposition to Freud's libidinal theory was that she saw neurotic disturbances as the outcome of relational disturbances, sexual or non-sexual. She could see that a patient can be a well sexually functioning individual but carrying neurotic conflicts; and this is where she highlighted the fundamental error of the theory. Also, she divided inner conflicts into healthy and neurotic. Healthy conflicts can usually be resolved and can even be entirely conscious, whilst neurotic conflicts are always deeply repressed, with higher severity, and involve a dilemma that feels insoluble.

When the caregivers handle the baby in pathogenic ways that create neurosis (e.g. overprotectiveness, perfectionism, inconsistency, neglect, etc.), the latter functions with basic anxiety to manage the frightening and untrustworthy world around them. They seek safety in one of the following exaggerated characteristics of their basic anxiety: helplessness (with *moving towards people* and extreme desire for protection as its neurotic solution), aggressiveness (with *moving against people* and attempting domination as its neurotic solution), and detachment (with *moving away from people* and avoiding the other as its neurotic solution). These three neurotic solutions also tend to be inflexible and compulsive.

In Horney's theory psychopathology rises out of a vicious circle in which the individual develops an *idealised image* as a response to the previously mentioned repressed aspects of their neurotic personality and of their inner conflicts. This idealised image creates some unattainable standards that either knock down the individual or create a sense of shrinking and alienation from the true self (*self-contempt*). This kind of inner conflict is for Horney the most serious one and why she talks about the *tyranny of the shoulds*.

Horney's criticism of Freud's perspective on female sexuality was respected and referenced even by him. She objected to the masculine standards that dominated psychoanalytic thinking of her time, and she asked how that had failed to present the real nature of women. She introduced the term *womb envy* for men to describe the equivalent of *penis envy*. This is when men feel envious of women's biological functions that they cannot have (e.g. pregnancy or breastfeeding), which is an expression of their fear of lack of control or diminished power. She also further explained penis envy for girls as something understandable given the narcissistic shame of having less than the boy and the manifest anatomical privileges of having a penis. For Horney this is the *primary penis envy* that occurs in girls before they know their childbearing capacity. The *secondary penis envy* appears in adult women and is all the feelings and experiences that have been miscarried in their development towards womanhood. This is where Horney also introduced the term *flight from womanhood* – women take masculine roles not because they desire to possess a penis, but because they feel anxious and guilty about having desires and libidinal energy towards the father. She adds that the deeper reason for this inner process, though, is women's disadvantaged position in society, a strong part of the reality that most women might not even be aware of. So, the constant inferiority imposition by society stimulates women's masculinity complex.

Fromm also reviewed Freud's theory under his Marxist lens, and his approach was called *humanistic psychoanalysis*. His initial take was that there was indeed a punitive superego that he characterised as paternalistic, but there was also a maternal conscience that embodied unconditional acceptance and tolerance. Later on, though, he moved away from the libido theory. He also argued that human development continues into adulthood, albeit with less intensity as external influences no longer have a big impressionable effect.

For Fromm, society plays a major role in human development. He sees humans as intricately connected to nature but they are also set apart from it because of their superior intellect. A proof of this is the sense of isolation and anxiety that exist in humans. Humans are characterised by reason, imagination, and self-awareness, and as they struggle to create their place in the world, they are motivated by learnt *non-organic drives*. These are as follows:

(1) *The need for others*: Fromm saw humans as primarily social beings and postulated that any kind of research on individual psychology is actually on social psychology. He described *mature love* and loving as an interpersonal creative capacity that secures firm roots in the world. His seminal work *The Art of Loving* is a succinct summary of his view on loving as an active and authentic form of caring for the loved person's life and growth. In this notion he also added the sense of responsibility towards humanity. Reaching the potential for loving is not given, and here he makes connections with primary narcissism and potential developmental stuckness in that.

(2) *Transcendence*: humans' need to go beyond the basic stages given by nature to push them to transcend and have an impact in their world. The fulfilment of one's potential is not easy as it depends on the important adults in the baby's life and on society. Besides the main aggressive quality required for survival (*benign aggression*), a baby can also develop some sort of non-organically motivated destructive attitude (*malignant aggression*) as a response to pathogenic parental behaviours and/or societal discrimination and neglect.

(3) *Identity*: this is what Fromm calls 'I am I' which comes as a combination of the growing baby relating to others but also recognising their separateness. It can be a confusing balance between dependence to have safety and to survive and independence to have freedom. When the growing baby starts becoming independent from the authority of their caregivers, it consequently starts feeling more isolated and anxious, connecting in this way

their freedom from restrictions with the freedom from the security and protection provided by the caregivers.

(4) *Frames of orientation*: this is the set of values and goals in the individual's life as a means to make meaning of the world. *Biophilia* is a healthy frame of orientation as the individual focuses on love, productivity, and reason. At the same time Fromm postulated that the need for an integrated and unifying personal philosophy is so desperate that even an irrational framework will do, instead of nothing. Under the umbrella of irrational and unhealthy frames of orientation we can see *necrophilia* (love of death), narcissism, dependence, the mechanisms of defence, the *receptive* orientation (a person who tends to seek love and nurture by others all the time), the *exploitative* orientation (a forceful person striving to obtain rewards), the *hoarding* orientation (a person seeking compulsive orderliness and characterised by obstinacy), and the *marketing* orientation (a person who sees themselves as a commodity and adjust completely to what the others want them to be, losing in this way their way towards self-realisation). A person can mix healthy and unhealthy frames of orientation.

Fromm saw the route of inner conflicts in the *escape* aspect of human nature towards freedom (another aspect is *embracing freedom*). As an attempt to alleviate isolation and alienation, humans choose certain escape mechanisms.

Psychopathology is seen as the result of either pathogenic parental behaviours or of the actual culture and society in which the individual lives and develops; both can block the drive for self-realisation.

Fromm saw community re-gathering and solidarity as the only possible way to repair humans' relationship with the world (in his notion of the 'world' he included the other-than-human as he was an advocate opposing environmental destruction, war, and poverty). He was one of the founders of 'socialist humanism' and saw psychoanalysis in this way too. Part of this view was also his support of the analyst's honesty and engagement in the analytic process as a reparative internalisation in contrast to the world's alienation and use of lies.

JACQUES LACAN, LINGUISTICS, AND POST-STRUCTURALISM

Lacan has been named as the 'French Freud' to represent his own desire for a return to Freud. As a contemporary Freudian revisionist, though, he took a postmodern turn and his work is characterised as post-structuralist. This is because he questioned the notions of the *self* and *truth* and saw knowledge as a construct based on linguistic and ideological structures; these, according to Lacan, are the organisers of both conscious and unconscious processes in life.

Therefore, he deviated from the Freudian bodily causes of behaviour and focused on the ideological structures that, especially through language, build people's understandings of their relationships with themselves and with others.

His theories borrowed elements from a very wide range of fields: from topology and mathematics to philosophy, anthropology, surrealism, and linguistics. Lacan strived to understand the human subject as a social phenomenon and that led him to Lévi-Strauss's cultural anthropology and Saussure's structural linguistics. As we will see next, Lacan went against the dominant Western ideology of his times that defined self-realisation as something an individual can achieve outside society.

Deviations from Freud: 'The unconscious is structured like a language'

Starting with this famous aphorism we can understand how language was Lacan's main lens to see and understand human subjectivity. For him human subjectivity cannot be present at birth as it is the result of a structuring path through relational experiences. Also, there cannot be an autonomous ego if we consider that we become human through unconscious symbolic processes expressed through language. Language, therefore, is for Lacan the determinant dimension in human experience. Neither self nor important relationships are the main pillars of the construction of human subjectivity as it was postulated by his predecessors. This was a rather uncompromising position and one that pre-empts Lacan's radical revision of the Oedipus complex and the structure of the psyche.

Psychical structure

For Lacan the psyche is structured by the mutually dependent elements of *the imaginary, the symbolic*, and *the real*; the latter is seen as the core of the triad whilst the other two are seen as inseparable and intertwined in their work and in tension with *the real*.

- *The real*: this is a state of nature that is associated with fullness or completeness. It is lost though when the infant enters the world of language. It is concerned with need.
- *The imaginary*: this is the psychic field of equations and identifications (see the second developmental stage next). It is primarily narcissistic and is concerned with demand.
- *The symbolic*: language and narrative are its contents (see the third developmental stage next). It is what connects subjects together in one action and is concerned with desire.

Since, according to Lacan, we are shaped and determined by socio-linguistic structures and dynamics, we can see how the imaginary is dependent on the symbolic and how the real is something that exists beyond language, beyond expressibility. Also, in simplistic terms, the imaginary represents the cultural trends and the symbolic the social laws.

Subjectivation is the process that creates the subject, where according to the symbolic order the identity of each subject is engraved with institutional and ideological force. The paradoxical nature of subjectivation can be understood if we consider the need and acquisition of a coherent self-image by the subject, whilst at the same time uncritically identifying with the social order that contains asymmetrical power, oppression, and injustice.

Lacan's rejection of human subjectivity as present at birth and his belief that it is socially and relationally constructed have supported the feminist psychoanalytic theories of female subjectivity as a social construct, as well as the more psychological and sociological theories about biology no longer being destiny.

What is your perception of language in connection with how you experience yourself, feel and express yourself?

Do you see symbolism as part of your verbal or non-verbal expression?

What gravity have you given to society, institutions, and ideologies in the formation of your identity?

The three developmental stages and the revised Oedipus complex

Lacan saw the infant going through three developmental stages that culminate in the crisis of the Oedipus complex that for him had nothing to do with the fear of biological castration, but it was more about the infant's self-perception and the beginning of their estrangement from their original self.

(1) First is the elemental period of unconscious infantile desire.

(2) Then, the *mirror stage* gives the infant their first challenge as they have to confront their image for the first time and in a narcissistic way – and incorrectly – assume that this is their true self. The *imaginary* emerges here.

(3) The *symbolic* order arises around the age of 2 years old when the child begins to acquire language and finds themselves in a crisis in their development with the first elements of self-awareness. This is where the *no(m) du père* (the name/no of the father) symbolises the beginning of the awareness of separation as the father here combines the roles of the separator of mother and child, ego ideal, and potential castrator. The effects of the *mirror stage* are epitomised here as the child sees themselves objectified and dependent on the other, *the third term*, and especially the father who is outside the existing mother–infant dyad. Alienation and self-estrangement start here, as the mother introduces the child into the social order of regulations and symbolic relationships.

As the self-system is constructed through *reflected appraisals* of others, Lacan postulates that the subject creates an adaptive self-perception that serves their security needs but that also restricts a richer and more satisfying existence.

Desire

For Lacan the term *desire* has a completely different meaning compared to other psychoanalytic theories. Lacanian desire has very little to do with sexual impulse, is different from needs, and portrays a wish to be everything; first for the mother and, later on, for the other. With this term he also highlighted the importance of a more existential longing, one that seeks reparation and is perpetually unfulfillable; therefore, one can never be themselves.

The analytical process and the heresy of the variable duration sessions

Lacan's view of the analytical process cost him his membership with the recognised international psychoanalytic societies. For him analysis was concerned with the dispersal of ordinary subjectivity (see also his involvement with the several socio-political causes of his time), with the discovery of the linguistic unconscious and the freeing from the petty everyday concerns and social relations, and with the exploration of desire through the symbolic order of language.

Free associations have the potential of unhinging the client from the burden of their ordinary subjectivity, needful attachments, and ego concerns. The analytic process, as a whole, aims to empower the clients' authentic voice so that they break through the ordinary constrictions of language. For Lacan psychoanalysis can transform the clients' relationship to language and can make the unintended meanings in their speech more explicable.

His view of the self as a social creation constructed out of reflections of the perspectives of others is the foundation of his analytic approach.

A heresy that contributed to the previously mentioned professional exclusion was his notion of variable duration sessions: a Lacanian-oriented session can last just five minutes. This was an incomprehensible deviation from the dependable routine of scheduled analytic hours and one that still makes Lacan's approach very different not only from other psychoanalytic and psychodynamic approaches but from the majority of psychotherapy approaches.

GETTING CLOSER: RELATIONAL PSYCHOANALYSIS AND THE INTERSUBJECTIVE MOVEMENT

The '80s and '90s found psychoanalysis searching for the deepened understanding of therapeutic relationships as mutually involving and mutually created (vs. the original psychoanalytic view of the analyst as a blank screen). That search created the fertile ground for the development of the *intersubjective systems theory* and of *relational psychoanalysis* in the USA, movements that have now expanded across all continents. During that period of expansion psychoanalysis appropriated several humanistic ideas without acknowledging them. So, I refer you to Chapter 4 to read more about humanistic psychotherapy and to discover its influences on psychoanalysis.

INTERSUBJECTIVE SYSTEMS THEORY

Based on phenomenology, intersubjective systems theory is a systems theory with an emphasis on the interaction of subjectivities in contexts. These are reciprocal and mutually influencing interactions, and the focus on them gives us some understanding of psychological phenomena.

George Atwood and Robert Stolorow introduced the term *intersubjectivity* to psychoanalysis and aimed to move meaning-making beyond intra-psychic and isolated mechanisms. Alongside Donna Orange, they theorised the process of relating and understanding psychological process within each intersubjective context – that is caregiver–child or analyst–patient. They postulated that early intersubjective patterns between caregivers and children have the potential for psychopathology.

The *subjective world* is seen as the contents of experience and *structures of subjectivity* as the constant principles that act as organisers of those contents in unconscious and recurrent ways and according to certain and distinctive themes.

This school of thought postulates that there are two forms of unconscious: the *pre-reflective unconscious* which acts as a shaping mechanism for experiences that fall outside a person's awareness, and the *dynamic unconscious* which encompasses blocked off affect states, the latter having failed to evoke attuned responsiveness in the individual's early environment.

Daniel Stern's work and research added extra layers of understanding intersubjectivity as he showed how human experience is not consistent but flows between moments of intense connectedness and of differentiation. He suggested that this kind of oscillation is present from the first months of a baby's life. For Stern the relationship between the mother's and the baby's subjectivities involves states of *interaffectivity*, those mutual regulations of affective experience within the dyad. *Affective attunement* also plays an important role in the intersubjective field between baby and mother – and, consequently, between patient and analyst – as the latter shows her ability to perceive her baby's behaviour and respond in a complementary manner. This sequence is then perceived by the baby.

Stolorow and Frank Lachmann have extended this sequence of inter-actions when they happen between an analyst and their patient. They postulate that within the intersubjective frame of working, the patient's experience of the analyst needs to be validated as the first assimilates their analyst's being and acting into their structures of subjectivity.

RELATIONAL PSYCHOANALYSIS

As a pluralistic collection of theoretical voices (see self psychology, interpersonal psychoanalysis, Ferenczi's approach, and object relations theories), relational psychoanalysis emerged out of and in reaction to classical psychoanalysis. The need to include intersubjective and interpersonal perspectives specifically in clinical work led Stephen Mitchell and later on several other USA-based psychoanalysts into a relational revolution regarding what the analyst knew and what the patient wanted. It is a radical field theory that includes not only the context of the patient's development and suffering but also the social field which is seen as powerfully interdependent with the individual. This two-person approach engages critically with Freudian drive theory and focuses more on establishing spaces of difference.

It is a collage theory of therapy rather than a theory of personality, and relational analysts bridge disciplines in an attempt to tame the tension between the aim of growth and the power of the past. The work of Daniel Stern, Beatrice Beebe, Lachmann, and the Boston Change Group stresses the importance of early dyadic life and early transactions in terms of future transformations, as well as stagnation.

The analyst's subjectivity and countertransference are strongly used, whilst the focus is on the patients' multiple self-states, shifts in identity states, and dissociative processes and with the aim of facilitating pro-found change in the clinical process. As a dialectical movement, it has altered the power dynamics in the clinical setting and has reviewed the importance of explicit and implicit self-disclosure from the analyst's side.

Some values and qualities common across the several relational psychoanalytic waves are as follows:

• Embodiment as a necessary ground to early memory, attach-ment and as a means of relational strategies
• Mutuality and maintenance of symmetry

- Active engagement from both sides of the dyad
- Negotiation around meaning and deviation from the absolute truth of the analyst's interpretations
- The analyst's vulnerability
- Authenticity and responsibility
- The inevitable uncertainty in the process

In relational psychoanalysis, the therapeutic relationship is seen as part of the general human relationships, and therefore, there is a focus on the many dimensions of relationality, as well as on the interplay between love and hate. The analyst is challenged to *surrender* to the emotional engagement to their patients with all the affect and intentionality, care, and empathy that that entails.

The bi-directional and mutual influence in the intersubjective field bring to light the importance of being recognised by another mind and the inevitability of enactments in clinical work. Intersubjectivity in this approach is a developmental process of capacity of the patient who experiences and learns from seeing the other as a complex subject in their own right, rather than a controllable or controlling object.

FEMINIST PSYCHOANALYSIS: TOWARDS A GENDER-CONSCIOUS PSYCHOANALYSIS

In the '30s and '40s classical culturalism emerged from within psychoanalysis, and Karen Horney and Clara Thompson opened the path for the feminist psychoanalytic movement. For them gender characteristics were cultural and social conditions, and the oedipal phase with its penis envy for girls and women was more about the realisation of differences in power and social constraints, arguing in this way, with Freud's original biologising of differences. In other words, these pioneers of deconstructing the patriarchal view of the Oedipus complex voiced the misplacement of the metaphor of penis envy and highlighted its actual meaning, the female envy of male power.

Since then, several feminist psychoanalysts have highlighted the patriarchal domination in Freud's views, especially in regard to female sexuality as expressed in the Oedipus complex.

This feeling and counter-thought led to the development of feminist ideas within psychoanalysis and the movement towards a more gender-conscious practice. Feminism also influenced the emergence of the two-person stance. This is where in analysis the two subjectivities emerge equally, and the analytic encounter is a mutually created reality (parallel to the feminist achievement of looking at the world from both the male and the marginalised perspectives).

Feminist psychoanalysis has been developing feminist principles in clinical practice and focuses on exploring femininity – the way one becomes and is not born a woman – as this is constructed in patriarchal cultures. The '60s and '70s found psychoanalysis further shifting from its one-person psychology and into a social psychology where the personal and the political were bridged. The work of Latin American feminist psychoanalysts – such as Laura Achard de Demaria in Uruguay or Marie Langer in Argentina – are vivid examples of this shift.

In the Western world, theorists like Jessica Benjamin gave attention to the mother's subjectivity in the intersubjective field between mother and baby. The mother is no longer seen as just an object for the baby, and there are possibilities of both recognition and identification of her as a subject. Their general critique of object relations theory, especially Winnicott's work, has led to the view of the mother's psychology in all its complexity, her view as a social being, and her occupation of simultaneously different or contrasting positions in the upbringing of her children, especially her daughters. These critiques emphasise that the development of infant psyche is connected to the complex and articulated psychology of their mother.

Other influential feminist psychoanalysts include Nancy Chodorow who stressed the pre-oedipal relationship between mother and child and the development of the self in relation to others, Jean Baker Miller and Carol Gilligan who emphasised the cultural view on different attributes for women and men, and the theorists in France – for example Joyce McDougall and Janine Chasseguet-Smirgel – who paid attention to the nature of female identity.

RECOMMENDED READING

Bateman, A., & Holmes, J. (2022). *Introduction to psychoanalysis: Contemporary theory and practice* (2nd ed.). London: Routledge.

Mitchell, S., & Black, M. (2016). *Freud and beyond: A history of modern psychoanalytic thought* (2nd ed.). New York: Basic Books.

REFERENCES

Atwood, G., & Stolorow, R. (1979/1993). *Faces in a cloud: Intersubjectivity in personality theory*. Northvale, NJ: Jason Aronson Inc.

Barsness, R. (Ed.). (2018). *Core competencies of relational psychoanalysis*. London: Routledge.

Ferguson, A., & Gutiérrez-Peláez, M. (2022). *Sándor Ferenczi: A contemporary introduction*. London: Routledge.

Fromm, E. (1942/1997). *The fear of freedom*. London: Routledge.

Gomez, L. (1997). *An introduction to object relations*. London: Free Association Books.

Karpf, F. (1953). *The psychology and psychotherapy of Otto Rank*. New York: Philosophical Library.

Midgley, N. (2013). *Reading Anna Freud*. London: Routledge.

Moore, B., & Fine, B. (Eds.). (1990). *Psychoanalytic terms and concepts*. New Haven, CT: The American Psychoanalytic Association.

Quinn, S. (1987). *A mind of her own: The life of Karen Horney*. New York: Summit Books.

Rustin, M., & Rustin, M. (2017). *Reading Klein*. London: Routledge.

Schwartz, J. (1999). *Cassandra's daughter: A history of psychoanalysis*. New York: Viking.

Stolorow, R. (2013). Intersubjective-systems theory: A phenomenological-contextualist psychoanalytic perspective. *Psychoanalytic Dialogues*, *23*(4), 383–389. https://doi.org/10.1080/10481885.2013.810486

3

COGNITIVE BEHAVIOUR THERAPY (CBT)
THE 'MARRIAGE' OF BEHAVIOUR AND COGNITION

CBT is an umbrella term that encompasses a number of approaches as we will see in this chapter. It is an ever-expanding and broad movement of therapies that vary in their formulations and emphases in treatment but nevertheless have some shared characteristics. These approaches seek to identify and replace maladaptive behaviours, cognitions, and feelings, and they do so from a strong base of scientific empiricism. They are also characterised by action orientation and present focus. The latter is a crucial aspect to the approach when we consider that CBT aims to help clients modify their current maladaptive thoughts in order to soothe their emotional upheaval. According to CBT approaches any intervention on historical factors would be pointless as these cannot be modified.

The journey of the formation of the CBT umbrella of therapies begins with behaviourism and behaviour therapies, continues with cognitive therapies, and progresses to the third wave CBT therapies with their more integrative and relational attitude. This is a journey that started with the success of empirical research by the behavioural approaches but later included thoughts, beliefs, imagery, and interpretations into the practice and research as the limitations of the focus on behaviour only became increasingly prevalent. Let's now look at this journey in more detail.

DOI: 10.4324/9780367824334-4

How did you hear about CBT for the first time (e.g. mentioned by your General Practitioner – GP, on social media, through reading)? What image do you have of the CBT approach?

BEHAVIOURISM AND BEHAVIOUR THERAPY

Behaviourism has its roots in Ivan Pavlov and John Watson's work who were Freud's contemporaries. Pavlov's experiments with dogs defined the widely used psychological term of *classical conditioning*, whilst Watson's work promoted behaviourism as a psychological school and was focused on external forces. Classical conditioning is a psychological process that happens when a conditioned stimulus (e.g. a bell ringing) is paired with an unconditioned stimulus (e.g. food). The unconditioned response to the unconditioned stimulus is a reflex response (e.g. salivation), so when the pairing is repeated a number of times, the individual develops a conditioned response (e.g. salivation and hunger) to the conditioned stimulus (e.g. a bell ringing) when the latter is presented. In other words, the conditioned response is learned through experience (I refer you to Pavlov's experiments with dogs for more information and detailed examples).

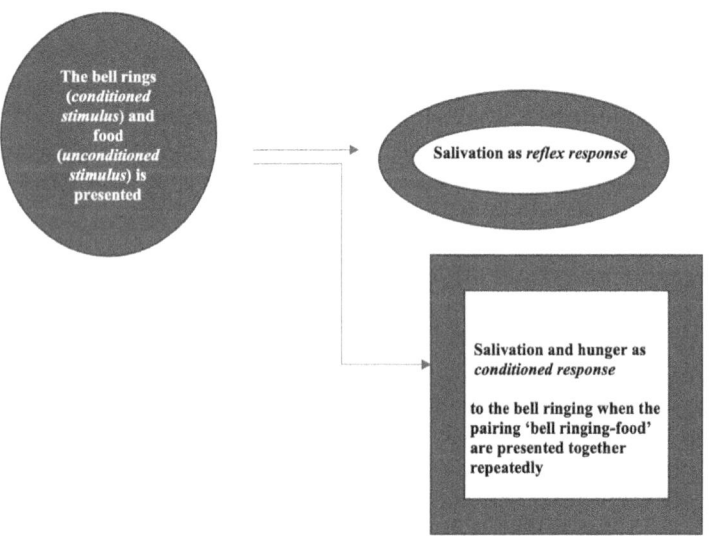

Sequence of stimuli and responses

Fast forward to the '50s, and we find Burrhus Frederic Skinner continuing the tradition of eliminating the image of the human as experiencing subject and concentrating on objective and measurable reality. This approach has been referred to as *radical behaviourism*. Skinner and his contemporaries looked for reproducible associations between stimuli and responses to explain humans' learning and behaviours. Skinner, more specifically, was very emphatic in his rejection of inner causes for behaviours and devoted his work to the understanding of the ways in which external variables shape and control human behaviour. He saw the environment as a continuous influencer on the individual; in other words, present actions are important for behaviour determination. Personality is then seen as consisting of the individual's behaviour repertoire that has built up over the years.

Skinner goes on to claim that all human behaviour is determined by prior conditioning, whether that is classical conditioning or, as in the concept he developed, *operant conditioning*. According to Skinner, our genetic endowment is responsible for the processes of operant conditioning where behaviours that act as effect producers are *reinforced* and more likely to occur in the future. Behaviour is then seen as a consequence of environmental histories of reinforcement. Therefore, the goal of scientific psychology is to predict and control future behaviours by finding the tools to *alter behaviour*. Maladaptive behaviours have environmental causes and are the result of poorly controlled, misplaced, or lost reinforcements. Therefore, any therapy input would be concentrating on facilitating alternative and adaptive behaviours via the use of positive reinforcement and the elimination and erasure of undesirable behaviours.

Under the umbrella of behaviourism we also find *eclectic behaviourism* represented primarily by John Dollard, Neal Miller, and Albert Bandura. Dollard and Miller tried to synthesise the two extremes of Freud's and Pavlov's theories with the use of clinical observations and experimental research, whilst Bandura paid attention to observational learning and emphasised the importance of cognitive causes of behaviour – opening up in this way the path for the development of cognitive therapies as we will see later on in this chapter.

More specifically, Dollard and Miller continued the theories on reinforcement which they postulated as operating outside one's awareness. For them therapy is about enabling clients to reduce their irrational fears, to abandon repression and all its harmful effects, and to start a journey of developing and applying their higher mental processes for the solution of problems. At the same time, they emphasised the process of bringing unconscious material to consciousness and believed in the concept of *drives* and Freud's theory that our basic motivation is to reduce various drives; however, they divided drives into *innate* (e.g. hunger) and *learned* (e.g. fear).

Bandura, on the other hand, argues that awareness is essential for any reinforcement to be effective. He saw humans as prone to act in ways that either produce expected rewards and/or avoid punishment; therefore, reinforcement involves a change in one's conscious anticipations. He coined the term *reciprocal determinism* to explain the process in which environmental influences, behaviours, and internal personal factors (e.g. beliefs and expectations) act as interlocking regulators for each other. Bandura also made an important contribution to developmental psychology and theories with his concept of *modelling/observational or social learning*. Learning by observing one's environment and how people behave constitutes the majority of their learning.

Behaviour therapy is the 'therapy child' of behaviourism as an academic discipline. It developed in the '50s as a reaction to the dominance of psychoanalysis since the late 19th century and is based on the theories by the previously mentioned behaviourists. It is a therapy discipline characterised by structure, directive attitude, empirically based interventions, and problem-solving focus and is mainly short term. The most prominent behaviour therapists of this second wave of therapies were Arnold Lazarus, Joseph Wolpe, and Hans Eysenck.

Lazarus developed *multimodal therapy* (MMT) and is credited with coining the term behaviour therapy. According to his approach a therapist needs to address the multiple modalities of an individual's *BASIC I.D.* (i.e. Behaviour, Affect, Sensation, Imagery, Cognition, Interpersonal relationships, and Drugs/biology). Any treatment needs to be tailored to each person's needs as they experience the effects of each personality dimension in a unique way. For Lazarus the individual is the result of their genetic history, physical environment, and social learning, and both classical and operant conditioning play a central role in the personality. His dissatisfaction with the stimulus-response behavioural explanations led him to appeal for a more eclectic view of human behaviour that was then interpreted in more depth by the cognitive therapists.

Wolpe's work was mainly focused on finding more effective ways of treating anxiety. His work developed from *reciprocal inhibition techniques* to *systematic desensitisation*. The first were techniques based on assertiveness and targeted anxiety that was inhibited by another feeling or response, not compatible with anxiety. His exploration of these techniques led him to the discovery of the well-known and widely used *systematic desensitisation* that involves a gradual exposure of the client to the anxiety-producing stimulus until the client no longer feels any anxiety towards it (e.g. systematically exposing a dog-phobic client to a dog).

Eysenck continued Lazarus's focus on personality and reshaped the concept of neuroticism, postulating that it was a biological form of emotional instability. He was notorious for his controversial views and research that connected personality with genetics as he was advocating a racialised view on intelligence that shaped the racist views on genetics. His theory focuses on the two central factors of extraversion (E) and neuroticism (N), which create the two axes of extraversion–introversion and neuroticism–stability. These axes then define certain basic personality types: *choleric* (high N and high E), *melancholic* (high N and low E), *sanguine* (low N and high E), and *phlegmatic* (low N and low E).

If you were to think of one of your senses, can you identify one that gets activated and produces feelings in the same way each time it is stimulated by a certain experience?

What do you think you are saying to yourself when you declare that you 'want to change your behaviour'?

What importance have you given to modelling of behaviours – to you and from you – over the years and in different settings?

THE SECOND WAVE OF BEHAVIOURAL THERAPIES

In the mid-'50s a new wave of theorists emerged within behaviour therapy. These were the theorists who questioned how cognitions could be treated in their own right, and how, therefore, they could be conditioned and deconditioned. The works of Aaron Beck, Albert Ellis, Donald Meichenbaum, and George Kelly gained more attention in the '70s, a period of 'cognitive revolution' for therapy and psychology, and consequently several cognitive behavioural therapies were developed. During that phase, behaviour therapy merged with cognitive therapies and CBT became the dominant term. This merging also ushered in a more democratic view of the relationship between client and therapist. The representatives of this wave focused on how thoughts can affect perceptions and consequently how one behaves.

Beck is considered the father of CBT and his and Ellis's theories have been the most influential in the formation of the core CBT principles that then became the base from which several other developments have emerged. They represent the *rationalist* approaches as they perceived the distorted worldviews as the source of psychological disturbance. At the other end of the CBT spectrum are the *constructivist* theorists who see each individual as an active constructor of their own world and include a more developmental component. Meichenbaum and Kelly belong to this second category.

Beck and Ellis have also acknowledged the significant influence of the Stoic philosophers, and more specifically Epictetus, on their view of the individual subjectively constructing reality and creating their own meaning to events. In CBT this is translated as clients actively clinging onto their disturbed philosophies about life and suffering as a result.

Let's now attempt a summary of the core shared CBT principles, assumptions, and concepts, followed by a brief description of the work of all four founding theorists.

Summary of shared principles, assumptions, and concepts

The practice of CBT is characterised by structure, action, and problem-orientation. It is a collaborative approach where client and therapist function as a team to overcome identified problems and is mainly time-limited and brief. All CBT approaches are also empirically based.

Starting from the premise that thoughts, feelings, and behaviours are interconnected, the goal of CBT is to modify thinking patterns through realistic evaluations so that the corresponding feelings and behaviours can improve and the individual can experience a longer-lasting overall psychological enhancement. In other words, a cognitive behaviour therapist teaches their client to learn to identify and then modify their dysfunctional thought processes, negative thoughts, and problematic perception of events that are underlined by irrational beliefs and assumptions, acquired since one's early development. These need to be restructured in order to see any demonstrable relief of symptoms. The irrational beliefs are also responsible for one's erroneous self-concept.

One's fundamental beliefs are held at a deep and core level of their personality and are called *schemata*. Any *schema deactivation* frees energy for the client to alter their self-perception, develop new strategies, explore different perceptions, and try out new behaviours and thoughts.

The interpretations one makes of situations are called *automatic thoughts (ATs)* and they influence their reaction on an emotional, behavioural, and embodied level. They are often connected to maladaptive underlying beliefs that the individual has about themselves, other people and/or the world and can also be inaccurate or unhelpful, especially if some kind of psychopathology intervenes in the process. Beck first introduced the term *negative automatic thoughts (NATs)* to describe the negatively coloured interpretations of what happens around or within the individual. Here a cognitive behaviour therapist is tasked to teach their client to recognise their NATs, to self-observe and identify triggers for these, to assess their impact, and, eventually, to modify them so that there is symptom relief/prevention. The next step in therapy is to explore the underlying schemata which prompt these NATs. NATs are responsible for negative emotional states, and the combination of negative thoughts and feelings becomes an obstacle in one's attempt to explore solutions.

Another important concept in connection to ATs and schemata is the *underlying assumptions (UAs)* that bridge the gap between the two first. UAs are the response to schemata and when they actually hinder the individual, they are called *dysfunctional assumptions (DAs)*. Schemata are seen as one's lens through which they perceive what happens, whilst UAs are the rules, conditions for living and being.

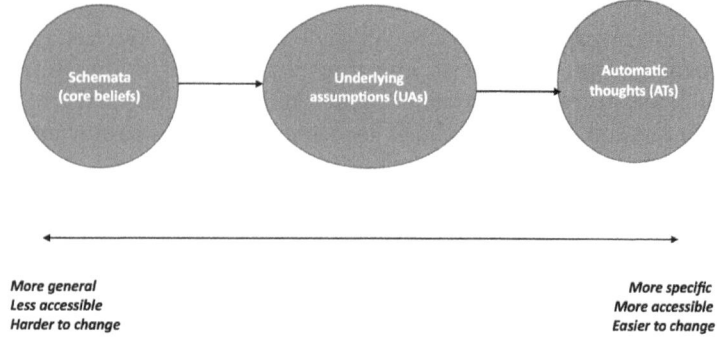

From schemata to automatic thoughts

Finally, in CBT there are the *perceived* problems (i.e. the reason for referral to therapy, the most distressing ones) and the *underlying* or *intermediate* problems that cause the perceived problems (i.e. the irrational beliefs about the self, relationships, the world). The problems are evaluated on the continuum between 'normal' emotional reactions to life events and extreme emotional reactions – usually in cases with some sort of psychopathology.

> How often do you refer to your 'rational self' or ask for someone to be more rational?
> In today's world, do you feel there is any focus on citizens' active participation in creating their environment and meaning of it?
> Have you ever thought what the underlying problem might be when a friend says that they find it difficult to maintain contact because of attention problems?

BECK'S COGNITIVE THERAPY (CT)

Beck developed CT as a response to his despair when treating patients with depression who wouldn't respond to the existing psychiatric and psychodynamic approaches. The breakthrough of his theory and therapy approach came in the mid-'70s when his research trials for the treatment of depression showed that CT was as effective as anti-depressant medication. Beck saw depression as a form of *thought disorder*.

CT is a structured and present-oriented therapy, initially for depression, but it has since been developed and applied to other diagnoses. It is often, and confusingly, referenced as CBT too, and it is characterised by continuous and extensive research as Beck was one of the world's leading researchers on psychopathology.

Apart from CT, Beck also developed the widely used *Beck depression inventory (BDI)*, a self-report measure for depression, and several other inventories (e.g. the *Beck hopelessness scale* or the *Beck anxiety inventory (BAI)*).

Beck's CT was based on the idea of *tapping the internal communications* – the therapist eliciting the client's thoughts that lie between an external stimulus and an emotional response, and then helping them understand the reasons for their reactions. Each event is interpreted by individuals in different ways and, therefore, their emotional response will be different too. Emotional responses depend on the severity of the impact of the event on the individual's *personal domain*, the cluster of real and abstract things that the individual considers important in their lives.

According to Beck, *schemata* are created early in childhood. So maladaptive schemata are created potentially from the time of one's birth, and they have to do with biased or distorted information-processing that leads to maladaptive assumptions about one's self, the world, and the future. NATs in adulthood are the result of the re-activation of early maladaptive schemata after a life event or stressor. If an individual does not have early maladaptive schemata, then stressors do not have such an impact on them and, thus, depression would not be the outcome.

Beck postulated that there are four major modes of interpretation of events that have an impact on an individual's self-esteem:

(1) Gain: pleasurable experience and anticipation of future satisfaction.
(2) Loss: experience and/or expectation of sadness and a desire to withdraw.
(3) Threat: the event activates the flight instinct. Anxiety and desire to avoid the situation are developed.
(4) Offense: the event is interpreted as a violation, so self-esteem is vulnerable. Anger, a need to secure self-esteem and/or to eliminate the threat develops.

This is the pattern: change in self-esteem because of an event → affect and motivation → behaviour → maladaption. If one of these four modes is repetitively activated, a reaction can become excessive and prolonged, and the individual can develop psychological disturbance.

The goals of CT are layered: first it's the relief of symptoms and problem resolution, then the acquisition of coping strategies followed by the modification of underlying cognitive structures that will empower the individual to prevent regressions. Beck found that better emotional health and the ability to modify behaviours came after the therapist's support towards the client to evaluate and change their distorted thinking. But for longer-lasting change and improvement he believed that the therapist's focus needed to be on the underlying beliefs.

ELLIS'S RATIONAL EMOTIVE BEHAVIOUR THERAPY (REBT)

Ellis's approach is defined by his attempt to highlight the role of irrational beliefs in everyday neurosis and the need to change these beliefs systematically and for the individual to learn to manage their consequent thoughts, feelings, and behaviours. The emphasis is on the evaluative – rather than the inferential – cognitive processes. The initial name of the approach, in the '50s, was *rational therapy*, but Ellis wanted to also include the feelings aspect of his approach so he later changed the name to *rational emotive therapy*. In the '90s he decided that all three elements of processing – cognitive, behavioural, emotive – needed to be represented, prompting him to once again change the name to *REBT*. Thus, we see that this theory is composed of these three factors at its core of understanding human functioning and dysfunctioning, and how the practice of this therapy is shaped by the interaction of these three factors.

The perception of the person in REBT is a hedonistic one, with a general desire to do well in life. The approach tries to help clients find an answer to how they prevent themselves from pursuing happiness and how they can find solutions to overcome any obstacles (e.g. irrational thoughts and beliefs, or irrational feelings). Here comes *rationality* in the shape of the support to the client to achieve their goals and as a flexible and consistent logical tool to deal with reality. This also connects to Ellis's belief that humans have the tendency, biologically, towards irrationality but also have an innate active tendency to work on fixing irrationality and pursuing their goals. REBT also has a strong element of self-acceptance and acceptance of the other as it is based on the notion of human complexity-fluidity and human fallibility.

Emotional disturbance in REBT is seen as a result of the individual's process of basing their views of unfortunate circumstances on their set of evaluative beliefs (i.e. the actual unfortunate circumstances are not responsible for any emotional disturbance). The *ABC model* is a core concept that explains this process:

A Activating event
B Beliefs associated with it
C Consequence – thinking, emotional, and behavioural

If one's beliefs (B) about an activating event or adversity (A) are dysfunctional and rigid, then the consequences (C) will probably be destructive on all three previously mentioned levels. Whilst if one's B are constructive and flexible towards the A, then the C will most likely be self-supporting.

MEICHENBAUM'S COGNITIVE BEHAVIOUR MODIFICATION (CBM)

Meichenbaum's theory attempts to understand the role of cognitive processes in coping with stressful situations, and more specifically how self-instructions might make a difference. In Meichenbaum's constructive integration of behaviour and cognitive theories, people's realities stem from their personal meanings and their own construction process. Maladaptive and harmful behaviours are the result of people's information processing, with all its cognitive errors and misperceptions that can distort reality. Meichenbaum sees cognitions as conditioned hidden behaviours that can be deconditioned and modified either via rewards or negative consequences. CBM can happen by several strategies (e.g. mental rehearsal or modelling) that engage the individual in an active way. Self-observation, changing negative self-talk to positive self-talk, and learning new skills are the three phases of CBM.

Meichenbaum developed the following techniques that have also been adopted by other approaches:

* *Self-instructional training*: this is a tool that involves homework practice where the client keeps a record of destructive and negative

self-statements and is then given training to replace those with healthy and adaptive self-talk.

- *Problem-solving technique*: when considering effective ways of dealing with life problems, a distinction can be made between the problem definition and the problem solution phase. Problem solving is seen as a tool (to solve the problem or achieve a goal), as well as a process (given that it involves a number of steps) and a skill (a lifelong one to deal with various problems and situations).
- *Self-management strategies*: these are a combination of cognitive and behavioural skills for the achievement of personal goals and the maintenance of self-motivation.
- *Stress inoculation training (SIT)*: this is a package of cognitive behavioural interventions introduced by Meichenbaum in the mid-'80s, which aims to prepare clients to handle stressful situations and events. Some of the techniques used in this package are problem solving, self instruction, relaxation, cognitive restructuring, and self-monitoring.

KELLY'S PERSONAL CONSTRUCT THEORY

Although Kelly himself didn't like being categorised as a cognitive theorist, his theory shares many elements with the CBT theoretical umbrella, but also with the humanistic one. His work emphasised the active role of individuals in constructing their own view of reality through experimentation (*man-the-scientist*) and in giving meaning to the world. Therefore, personal constructs for Kelly are the ways the individual gathers information, evaluates it, and in the end interprets it. Because of the individual nature of this process, there are differences amongst people who predict and explain events in their own unique way. This process also influences our personalities and the way we relate to other people and interact with our environment.

Kelly also introduced the idea of *constructive alternativism* to describe the fluidity of constructs. This means that the individual modifies their constructs constantly to fit with the reality or when they want to expand their repertoire to be better equipped to deal with new or difficult situations.

This constant motion in people's processing is also expressed in Kelly's *fundamental postulate* where he states that one's anticipation of events acts as a psychological channel for their processes. But sometimes the transitions from an ineffective construct to an effective one, that allows prediction and control of situations, might not be that easy and so the individual's difficulty in this process results in problems. These are manifested psychologically through fears, anxieties, guilt, or threats.

THIRD WAVE THERAPIES

This is the group of therapies that had their genesis in the '80s and represent the evolution of the second wave CBT approaches towards the achievement of more comprehensive life goals, an equal attention to thoughts and feelings, and with a view also of unifying with the dynamic therapies (i.e. psychodynamic and humanistic therapies). They share an emphasis on acceptance and mindfulness as a means of holistically promoting psychological and behavioural processes that contribute to one's well-being. They also consider more comprehensive goals, rather than only eliminating symptoms by changing behaviours, and focus more closely on the context, functions, and processes towards one's internal experiences. I will present here the approaches most widely researched and most represented in mental health services, but, as always in this book, this is not an exhaustive list of the many and constantly evolving therapy approaches of this kind. I also refer you to Chapter 5 and the section on 'Mindfulness-oriented psychotherapy' for some more examples on third wave approaches.

ACCEPTANCE AND COMMITMENT THERAPY (ACT)

Steven Hayes developed this approach as part of his own healing journey, and specifically his panic attacks. As an action-oriented approach it aims to facilitate development and expansion of clients' psychological flexibility in the form of openness, as well as thought and behaviour adaptation towards a better alignment of values and goals. Hayes highlights the importance of a pushback of cultural normativity in terms of fixing and changing 'negative' feelings. In ACT clients embody a different approach towards their inner feelings; one that pushes back any avoidance and denial and embraces a deeper acceptance towards their feelings and a commitment to behavioural change. Hayes talks about the acknowledgement of the appropriateness of 'negative' feelings as responses to certain situations, and, at the same time, the recognition that these feelings are not what stop the individual from moving forward.

For Hayes the necessary transformative shift in the way one looks at their 'negative' feelings requires acceptance, mindfulness, and values. At the same time psychological flexibility, that is the ability to remain grounded in the present despite any feelings, bodily sensations, and/or thoughts whilst in the process of choosing behaviours according to one's values and the situation, is promoted by the following processes:

- Acceptance of all thoughts and feelings
- Distancing one's self from and changing the way one reacts to distressing thoughts and feelings with the consequent moderation of any harmful effects (*cognitive defusion*)
- Being present and mindful of all thoughts and feelings without any judgement or effort to change them
- Seeing one's self as context and not identifying as just their feelings, thoughts, and experiences
- Choosing personal values and endeavouring to live according to them – as opposed to avoiding any emotional pain or meeting other people's/certain context's expectations
- Committing to taking action and encompassing in one's life those changes that align with their values and lead to positive change

COGNITIVE ANALYTIC THERAPY (CAT)

CAT stemmed from Anthony Ryle's effort to meet the high demand for therapy in an inner London National Health System service, and thus, he brought together analytic and cognitive practices to speed up the process and make therapy more widely available – whilst at the same time actively trying to grasp his clients' unconscious functions. It is a time-limited and active form of therapy that mainly focuses on relationship patterns, starting from the premise that early relational patterns shape many of the later automatic responses to other people and the way one relates to their own self.

As a collaborative model it emphasises the importance of (1) the client's active participation in the form of self-observation and acknowledgement of what needs to be changed, and (2) the therapist's empathic attitude towards the client so that the former can help the latter make sense of their emotional blocks and implement the required changes that can enable their self and relationships to blossom. Each therapeutic contract is tailored to the needs of each client and their own manageable goals, and they are encouraged to take part in the process of change in their own unique way, whilst also using creative means (e.g. drawing or movement) for self-discovery and self-reflection. Part of the process involves collaborative letter writing between client and therapist, based on the client's story and relational patterns. The development of diagrams and 'maps' of problematic and/or helpful patterns is also one of the collaborative techniques used in CAT.

The main emphasis of the approach is the understanding of patterns of maladaptive behaviours and the consequent enabling of the recognition of those patterns (thinking, feeling, and behaving), for understanding their origins, and then learning alternative ways to cope with them. It is an approach that aims to change the learned attitudes and beliefs about one's self and about others.

DIALECTICAL BEHAVIOUR THERAPY (DBT)

As an educational approach, DBT was originally developed by Marsha Linehan for the management of intense feelings, with a focus on self-destructive impulses – especially for chronic suicidal clients. An additional focus is the learning of negotiating skills for social relationships.

Because DBT deals with the experience of intense feelings, it has been used for client groups with diagnosed borderline personality disorder (BPD), post-traumatic stress disorder (PTSD), and any other kind of psychiatric classification that involves clients with emotional regulation difficulties or with a tendency for self-destructive behaviours (e.g. with disordered eating or substance use habits). It provides clients with tools to recognise and challenge any distorted thinking that underlies difficult feelings and encourages unproductive behaviour. At the same time, it is an approach that teaches clients to accept their problematic feelings – recognising that feelings are constantly changing and can sometimes be contradictory – and aims to empower them to make positive changes in their lives. Living in the present moment, regulating feelings, developing healthy ways to cope with life stressors, and developing skills to improve and maintain relationships with others are the main goals. These are achieved by practicing one's skills in the following areas: (1) mindfulness, (2) emotional regulation, (3) assertive interpersonal attitude, and (4) distress tolerance.

Linehan used the term 'dialectic' to describe the integration of opposites and their balance. Given the complexity of today's life, DBT tries to highlight the constant flow of things, including the non-static nature of one's health. A dialogical way of relating to one's self and to others allows for some balancing of the opposing forces, with the application of one's emotional and cognitive regulation that is achieved when they learn what triggers reactions to certain situations and emotional states. DBT teaches clients to assess situations and choose the most helpful coping skills to manage their thoughts, feelings, and behaviours – and to avoid any non-beneficial/intensely upsetting reactions.

DBT is practised in a group format with instructions and, at the same time, in individual therapy sessions on a weekly basis for six months to a year.

RECOMMENDED READING

Kennerley, H., Kirk, J., & Westbrook, D. (2017). *An introduction to cognitive behaviour therapy: Skills and applications* (3rd ed.). London: Sage.

REFERENCES

Beck, J. S. (2021). *Cognitive behavior therapy: Basics and beyond* (3rd ed.). New York: The Guilford Press.

Robertson, D. (2010). *The philosophy of cognitive-behavioural therapy (CBT): Stoic philosophy as rational and cognitive psychotherapy*. London: Karnac.

Trower, P., Jones, J., & Dryden, W. (2015). *Cognitive behavioural counselling in action* (3rd ed.). London: Sage.

4

HUMANISTIC PSYCHOTHERAPY
THE THIRD FORCE?

When Abraham Maslow was gathering all rebellious psychology and psychotherapy forces in the early 1950s, he must have felt a little bit like a Millennial against the Baby Boomers (i.e. psychoanalysis) and the MTV generation (i.e. behaviourism) that dominated the world and, specifically, the therapy field. On the one hand, there was Freud and his 'family' trying to analyse the inner conflicts of their patients' pathological selves; on the other hand, there were Watson and Skinner believing in the therapists' expertise for a transformation of human behaviour. Both psychoanalysis and behaviourism seemed to be constricting humans, reducing their inner processes into certain ways of being and being explained. In other words, there was a need to escape from the reductionist image of humans and to find ways for expansion and reaching out to the world and the other than human. Are we then talking about *humanistic psychology* as the third force in the therapy field or as a totally new paradigm that challenged both its predecessors as well as society with its solid beliefs on human potential?

Here I would like to make the following clarification regarding the use of the terms psychology and psychotherapy within a humanistic context: humanistic psychology is the academic term, and humanistic psychotherapy (or therapies as we will see in this chapter) the clinical one. From now on I will be using the term

DOI: 10.4324/9780367824334-5

'humanistic psychotherapy' as it more accurately represents the focus of this book.

From the mid-1940s Carl Rogers was sowing the seeds for a new view of human development by working on clinical subjects that would form the beginnings of this revolutionary approach. It was in 1954 when Maslow started a mailing list, gathering all the then thinkers who wanted to join their forces on the themes of *self-actualisation, creativity, and growth* – the latter included the belief in higher values and love. From then, and until the late 70s, humanistic psychotherapy thrived in a society that was trying to re-establish itself after the Second World War and its consequent financial implications and lack of opportunities. It's no wonder that the founders of the approach concentrated heavily on the notion of human potential and human achievement. The radical aspect of humanistic psychotherapy was the conscious attitude of reducing the therapist's power in the relationship with the client. The therapist was seen as a facilitator, a catalyst in the client's journey towards their growth potential rather than an expert authority.

The original umbrella of humanistic therapies included the *person-centered approach* (then client-centered psychotherapy), *Gestalt psychotherapy*, *transactional analysis*, and *existential psychotherapy*. In the early '60s *transpersonal psychology* was added to the family with Maslow co-founding this branch with Anthony Sutich in an attempt to study humans' highest potentials. *Encounter groups, co-counselling*, and *feminist therapy* were included in the humanistic family around the same time.

Core values and attitudes

- Self-actualisation, growth, and human potential: human nature is seen as fundamentally positive but not idealised or abstract. Therapy is more about growth rather than cure. Clients are self-empowered and are seen as knowledgeable participants of a co-created process.
- The human as a whole: mind–body–spirit are a union, and each needs the other in the process of personality development; none can stand on its own. One's mind–body continuum is not dichotomised, and spirituality is seen as a fundamental aspect for human growth.

- The power of the phenomena in the relating field: the 'healing through a meeting of two persons' emerges from a more ordinary way of communicating (vs. the psychoanalytic and behaviouristic models with their jargonistic languages). Contact, in the form of being with each other and maintaining this, is at the core of the relating field, which also encourages spontaneity and creativity as meaningful means of awareness and expression. Humanistic psychotherapy is after all an experiential paradigm, both in practice and in its research.
- Equality and critique of social norms and power: as a theory that stemmed from the critique of the existing theories of personality development and of society, it wouldn't be congruent if it didn't include as its values the consistent critique of social norms and the notion of power in relationships. Equality is an essential value in the therapy process; thus, the receiver of therapy is called 'client' and not 'patient'; the therapist relates to them as equals and understands their troubles, being aware of any power struggle when the client is sometimes not capable of accessing their equal way of being in the relationship.

> How do you see the concepts and experiences of growth, one's potential, and creativity in today's world?
>   Is equality in the therapeutic relationship important for your choice of a therapist/therapeutic approach for training?
>   Have you considered the influence of power in therapy and the therapeutic relationship?

THE FOUNDING APPROACHES AND MASLOW'S LEGACY

MASLOW'S THEORY

The legacy of Maslow's theory looms large in so many fields other than psychotherapy. His model of hierarchy of needs, as well as the concepts of *self-actualisation* and *peak experiences*, has even been absorbed into our everyday language. Therefore, it feels necessary to sketch the basics of his theory before we look in detail at what the three founding approaches are all about.

Maslow's theory made a difference at the time as it concentrated on the healthy parts of individuals, unlike the contemporary focus in the field that was on psychopathology. We will see this focus in the theories of other humanistic approaches too, but it is important to hold this detail in mind as we progress through the theories in this book.

His *theory of human motivation* is a five-tier model that can be depicted in the shape of a pyramid (see how today we refer to Maslow's theory as simply Maslow's pyramid of needs although Maslow never depicted his theory in this way). Starting from the bottom up we have the four tiers of deficiency needs: physiological needs (e.g. food and clothing), then safety needs (e.g. shelter, employment), needs for love and belonging (e.g. friendship), esteem; whilst the final need of self-actualisation is described as a growth/being need. The idea is that we humans go through a series of behaviours and motivations with the aim of satisfying the first four tiers of needs – more or less, but not necessarily fully satisfying them – to meet our goal for self-actualisation, which comes from our desire to grow. Life events, though, do not guarantee a uni-directional movement of our needs, and we may find ourselves going back and forth through the hierarchy during the span of our lifetime.

Self-actualisation is best described by Maslow's words 'What a man can be, he must be'. It is about the individual reaching their full potential and then potential reaching *peak experiences* that give them an elevated sense of happiness and fulfilment. Maslow connects peak experiences with spirituality and reaching one's true self. Peak experiences include art making, sex, connection with nature, scientific achievement, introspection, etc.

THE PERSON-CENTERED APPROACH (PCA): IT'S NOT ALL ABOUT EMPATHY

Carl Rogers's theory of personality and therapy can be seen as influenced by and/or rooted in more than one philosophical tradition, with the existential and phenomenological paradigms being the most distinctive influences. Due to the radical nature of the PCA that derived from practice, it is difficult to pinpoint its philosophical paradigm. Nevertheless, even Rogers himself admits to being influenced by Søren Kierkegaard's existential writings; we see this when he uses phrases such as being 'the self one truly is' or that 'this is true for me but I realise it may not be true for a lot of other people'.

Another influence on Rogers's theory comes from his seminal dialogue with the existential philosopher Martin Buber. Although Buber's idea of the 'I–Thou' relationship (i.e. a subject – 'I' – treats another subject – 'Thou' – with uniqueness and mutuality) was explicitly referred to in Rogers's writings only shortly before his death, the important discovery for Rogers at that point is that it is not a simple 'I–Thou' mutuality – in the sense of equality – that matters when change occurs, but rather the degree of attunement between therapist and client and the change taking place in both parts of the therapy relationship.

Introduction of the notion of *change* takes us to features that the PCA shares with the phenomenological paradigm: the fundamental idea of 'the primacy of the experience' and the predominant role of the subjective element. It is lived experience that gives the clues to an understanding of a person and consequently to what happens in the therapeutic process. Rogers's 19 propositions for a fully functioning person are the foundation of his theory of personality and confirm the role of phenomenology when he talks about a 'continually changing world of experience' and the *perceptual field* which is each individual's reality.

Similarly, the Rogerian notion of the *individual frame of reference* parallels the phenomenological idea of subjective perception at any given moment. Perception is a core concept in the PCA, and this is highlighted by its inclusion in the six necessary and sufficient conditions of therapeutic change (see the six conditions later in this chapter). Also, the importance of individual autonomy and choice is at the heart of both the PCA and the phenomenological paradigms.

Continuing to review the philosophical influences on the PCA, we can also consider Karl Marx's influence on Rogers when thinking of the relevance of the idea of communism in society to the egalitarian aspect of the therapeutic relationship.

Person-centered therapy has undergone several name changes throughout its history: it was initially described as *relationship therapy*, changing into *non-directive therapy* (meaning the intention not to influence), and later into *client-centered therapy* before its final naming that I use in this book.

The tendencies and the self

PCA's theory of personality has been expressed in terms of *tendencies*, seen as innate. We could depict these as a bunch of balloons.

The biggest one is the *formative tendency*, the medium-sized one the *actualising tendency*, and the smallest one the *self-actualising tendency*. The size of the balloons shows the extent of each tendency in human personality. Another way to put it is what is contained in these three balloons illustrates one's journey from collective to individual functioning.

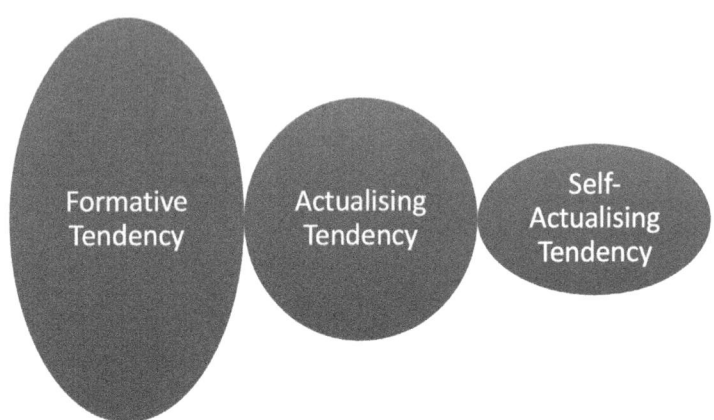

The tendencies

- *Formative tendency*: this is the tendency towards greater differentiation, complication, and integration through which more complex entities come up and creativity is empowered. Further definitions have included the concepts of *universal energy, interconnectedness of all things*, and *organic world*, highlighting the reference to both human and the other-than-human.

- *Actualising tendency*: springing from the formative tendency, the actualising tendency is that inner power in humans that pushes us to grow, invest in personality change, and achieve or fulfil our potential. It has been regarded as the foundation of the PCA and as fuelling a client's motivation for change. The actualising tendency was initially described by Rogers as an innate 'drive' common to all biological organisms. The word drive is not used in a Freudian manner but rather to give us the sense of the organism as proactive in the direction of growth and adaptation, as well as introducing the notion of autonomy. In all his writings, Rogers emphasised the triple action of this tendency in the human species: it actualises, maintains, and enhances the experiencing organism. From this triple function, we can see how, even in unfavourable conditions, the actualising tendency remains alive and constructive, as much as the environment allows; for interaction between organisms and their environment will determine whether there is positive development or inhibition of the drive. However, whatever the outcome, an organism will strive to develop.

- *Self-actualising tendency:* as a subsystem of the actualising tendency, the self-actualising tendency is a distinctly psychological form of the former related to the *self*. It involves the actualisation of that portion of experience symbolised in the self. It can be seen as a push to experience oneself in a way that is consistent with one's conscious view of what one is. Self-actualisation refers to the maintenance and enhancement of the self as a portion of the phenomenal field – not of the organism as a whole. At this point, it is important to highlight the self-actualisation links to the therapeutic process and to change generally. Whilst self-actualisation might be a means of increasing autonomy and independence, it does not imply separateness and alienation; we can even say that it promotes interest for, and empathy to, others.

The self and its components

The self is seen as connected with the actualising tendency and as 'the product of differentiation of some experiences and perceptions into an "I" or "me"'. The self is utterly related to the relationships around it and has a dual nature: it is fluid and changing but also organised and consistent.

Self is seen in the restricted sense of the awareness of being, of functioning and, if we include the self in the tendencies, we can see that it is a particular part of one's total experiencing. But in the PCA, there is also a more total and larger version of the self – called the *organismic self*. This self includes the experiencing self but is largely free of external constraints and therefore is the authentic self. This gives us a sense of tension between the restricted and the boundless self.

Returning from the organismic self to the experiencing self, we come across the *self-concept* or *self-structure*, the *ideal self*, and the *parts or configurations of the self*:

Self-concept or self-structure: the view one has of one's self exists in a counterbalance with the organismic self. The self-concept or self-structure has been seen as composed of perceptions of the self that have managed to come into awareness, as a conceptual construction of one's self. The self may be imagined as a sponge of rulings and introjects that strives to distinguish itself from the organismic self.

Ideal self: this is the self-concept the person would most like to have, the most desirable perceived person. The ideal self is often activated in the therapeutic process. Clients may be seeking to actualise this, but equally, they can be quite persecuted by the ideal self.

Parts or configurations of the self: a configuration of the self is a hypothetical construct, signifying a coherent pattern of feelings, thoughts, and behavioural patterns. It is symbolised – or pre-symbolised – by the person as a reflection of a certain existence within the self. Some configurations can also be perceived as adaptations to the introjection of particular conditions of worth (see next for more on this concept). In everyday life, we can see configurations of the self in action when, for example, we hear expressions like 'it was my angry self who talked to my manager like this'. These are parts of the self who take the form of behaviours and/or reactions. They can aid growth, but they can have negative effects as well.

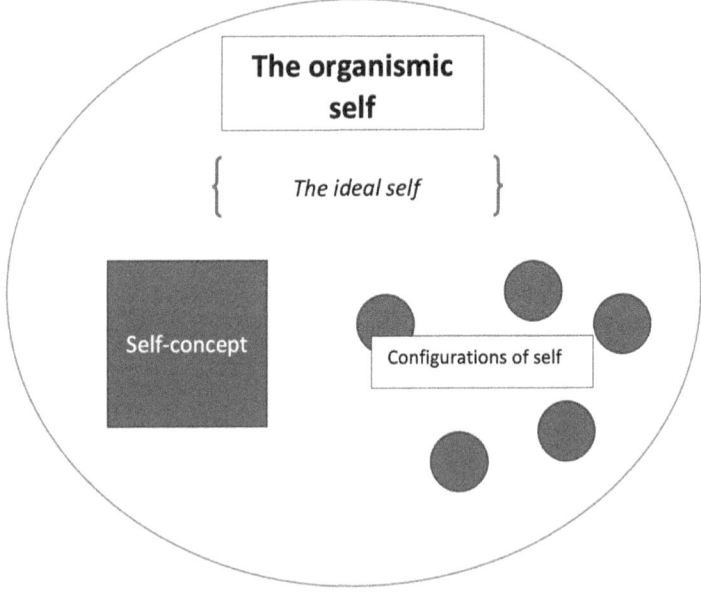

The organismic self

*Conditions of worth, unconditional positive regard, and defence
mechanisms: the person-centered theory of personality and development*

Connected to the development of the self-concept and self-actualisation are two related needs – assumed to be most likely experienced in childhood: the need for *unconditional positive regard* (UPR) from others and the need for *positive self-regard* – an internalised version of the former. These lead to the favouring of behaviour that is consistent with the person's self-concept. *Conditions of worth* are the cause for the difficult internal process a person goes through when they positively value only those experiences associated with positive self-regard and reject or avoid those that are not.

At the same time, the person who trusts their own inner experience builds up some positive self-regard, and this allows them to trust their own perceptions and evaluations of the world as they experience it. In other words, this person has an *internal locus of evaluation*. The opposite attitude of relying heavily on the values of others and, consequently, acting in a way that dismisses this internal evaluation of experience for the sake of the others' positive regard, leads the person to experiencing an *external locus of evaluation* and functioning under conditions of worth, the introjected values.

Conditions of worth are relational as human beings are essentially relational and deeply affected by our surrounding societal, cultural, gender, ethnic, and class norms. When our actualising tendency is nourished and we can trust our own feelings and thoughts which resonate with our own perceptions and desires, then a person's *organismic valuing process* is in good order and they can move on in their life. When the wisdom of one's organismic valuing process gets into a conflict with a desperate need for approval that might be of an opposite nature, we can then speak of submission to the conditions of worth. In such a state then the person feels threatened by the experience that causes these conflicted feelings and either distorts or expels them from their awareness.

Distortion and denial are the two main *defence mechanisms* one uses to try to smooth over the conflict between self-concept and experiences that do not fit with or promote the conditions of worth. Let's see, though, the process that leads to psychopathology:

(1) The person is in a significantly elevated state of incongruence between their self-concept and their actual experience. If a further experience takes place, which happens to highlight this

incongruence, then the organism's defence mechanisms have not functioned successfully.

(2) Next, there is an experience of anxiety as the incongruence starts to affect the person. The extent of the anxiety depends on how much of the self-concept is under threat.

(3) This is followed by an experience of dis-organisation caused by the failure of the defence mechanisms. The experience is accurately symbolised in conscious awareness, and often the self-concept has effectively broken under the pressure.

(4) Finally, the state of dis-organisation is experienced idiosyncratically either as anxiety, confusion, or pain or, in terms of psychopathology, perhaps as depression.

Here I would like to clarify that in the PCA the use of the term psychopathology is not used as it would be in the medical sciences (including psychiatry), but it is rather a description of some prolonged incongruence. It is the person's inability to process meanings and capacities in order to create more functioning alternatives, highlighting in this way the processing aspect of psychopathology as well as its intra-psychic and interrelationship aspect.

The ultimate aim in our development according to our actualising tendency is to reach a state of being fully functioning. This can be seen as a correlation of the degree of congruence between the organism and the self-concept. A fully functioning personality is also a process concept rather than an outcome. A fully functioning person is as follows:

• Open to experience, information, and learning to optimise growth and without any feelings of threat
• Able to listen and trust and is highly aware of their feelings, self, and others' feelings
• Capable of living in the here-and-now
• With a trust and confidence in their organismic valuing process
• Deeply connected to their own source of wisdom, without needing the others' approval

The six conditions for psychological change: the theory of therapy

The principle of non-directivity underpins the practice of the PCA in its classical form but also that of the real involvement of the client and the handling of power in the therapeutic relationship. The non-expert attitude by the therapist is complemented by their non-directivity; the intention is to not try to wrestle the change process away from the actualising tendency.

The six conditions for psychological change seem to rotate from relational (client–therapist) to individual (client or therapist), making us imagine the dyad working together, or the client as an independent unity, or the therapist as a separate and fully formed unity. At the same time the conditions are co-created in a cultural context that considers power and inequalities, whether those are structural and/or experienced.

Condition 1: being in (psychological) contact

This is the condition that highlights the importance of being in relationship, and it has to do with the influence taking place in the phenomenological and experiential field between the client and the therapist. Awareness of the other's presence is needed; therefore, contact is reciprocal and consensual.

Condition 2: when the client is and understands that they are incongruent

The client understands that something causes them to experience a problem in coping with conflicts between their conditions of worth and their actualising tendency and decides to see a therapist whom they trust will be able to help them. It is the state of feeling dissatisfied, in discomfort, distress, discontent with their life.

Condition 3: being congruent

Congruence is the therapist's state of being and their experience in relation and in response to their client. It is a very alive state, connected to the therapist's actualisation, and it does not need to be communicated verbally (i.e. through self-disclosure); it is realised through unconditional positive regard and empathy – the two following conditions.

Condition 4: unconditional positive regard

Unconditional positive regard is described as a central cohesive source of support and stability, for constructive change. It is the absence of judgement, the positive regard, warmth, respect, acceptance, valuing, and prising of the client by the therapist, who communicates all the previously mentioned through empathic understanding and consistency.

Condition 5: empathy

For the PCA the therapist is in a constant emotional – and cognitive – state of perceiving the client's internal frame of reference but without needing to understand and/or come to conclusions. The therapist puts themselves temporarily in their client's life scenario, in a subtle and sensitive way. The client feels understood, accompanied, and also valued by their therapist's empathy and kinaesthetic empathy (i.e. embodied movement demonstration of empathy), and together with their feeling of being accepted (see unconditional positive regard), they find a mirror in their therapist's responses.

Condition 6: the client perceives their therapist's empathy and unconditional positive regard

This last condition is an extra supporting element of the equality within the therapeutic relationship according to the PCA. It is not just about the therapist communicating their empathy and unconditional positive regard to the client but also the client needing to perceive these qualities for change to happen.

> When you think about your upbringing, which systems (e.g. family, education) do you think have conditioned your perception of your self most?
> What place does congruence/authenticity play in your experiencing of relationships and of yourself in them?
> Do you see a difference between empathy and sympathy?

Branches of the PCA as the family expands

In the development of new branches in the PCA there is a distinction between those that present a clear connection to classical client-centered therapy and to a set of core person-centered values in the therapeutic relationship (e.g. non-directivity), and those that add new ideas in an attempt to expand the existing theoretical thinking and its potential constraints:

- Relational/dialogical approaches: these are the developments in the PCA that put special – and main – emphasis on dialogue and the 'in between'. Dave Mearns's notion of *relational depth* has opened the way for a 'two-person-centered therapy' where the focus is on the therapist's facilitation of profound encounters with their clients and on a deep level. *Encountering* the client is at the core of Peter Schmid's dialogical approach – mainly influenced by Emmanuel Levinas's philosophical theories on the ethics of the Other.
- Focusing-oriented therapy: Eugene Gendlin, a colleague of Rogers, was the founder of this approach that explored the relationship between the individual's experiencing and how they express/symbolise/say it, bringing awareness into the mind–body continuum (see the term *felt sense* that describes the combination of a feeling as an emotion and as a bodily sensation).
- Experiential person-centered therapy: this is an approach that further developed Gendlin's theory and practice on experiencing. It highlights the importance of the client's wisdom in their mind–body, thus, the therapist needing to pay close attention to everything they share – verbal and non-verbal alike – as well as checking in with them as a means of maintaining contact in an empathic and egalitarian way. The dialogical and process-oriented way of relating within the therapeutic relationship is of more importance than the actualising tendency for the client's change and reclaiming of their desire to live.
- Person-centered expressive arts therapy (EAT): this approach was developed by Natalie Rogers, Carl Rogers's daughter, and it is an intermodal way of working with the client, using various arts – movement/dance, art, music/sound, writing, and drama – as well as imagery, improvisation, and meditation. The function of the arts is not for aesthetic purposes but rather for self-insight. N. Rogers also integrated concepts from analytical psychology, such as the inner polarities and the shadow (i.e. unconscious or unknown parts of the self).

- Pre-therapy: in an attempt to understand and establish contact with 'out of contact' clients, Garry Prouty developed pre-therapy as a set of concepts and practices. He described his work and theory as 'applied phenomenology' and highlighted the importance of restoring contact with certain clients, before actually trying to engage in therapy (thus the name pre-therapy).
- The integrative approach to person-centered therapy: Richard Worsley's concept of integration is based on a continuum from the classical approach to the experiential one, whilst also being open to new theories and ways of practising and with a consciously limited critical engagement.

GESTALT PSYCHOTHERAPY: ON SHAPING AND TRANSFORMATION

Frederick (Fritz) and Laura Perls were brewing their ideas and desire for theoretical change for a couple of decades before the seminal publication of the book *Gestalt Therapy* in 1951 and the founding of their first Institute of Gestalt Therapy in New York in 1952. The philosopher Paul Goodman worked alongside the couple and contributed to the very first book. Fritz Perls, though, seems to have been given the credit as the founder of Gestalt psychotherapy, which says a lot about how his restlessness and challenging attitude to therapy work have shaped some sort of stereotypical idea about what this approach represents (i.e. direct and challenging work).

Gestalt psychotherapy is influenced by both psychological and philosophical theories:

- Sigmund Freud: Fritz and Laura Perls were psychoanalytically trained, and they were inevitably influenced by the founder of psychoanalysis and his theories. Nevertheless, their approach is characterised as a radical revision of psychoanalysis as it challenges the idea of interpretation and the past. In Gestalt psychotherapy analysis is no longer the main focus; on the contrary, the integration of disparate parts, Ego awareness in the here-and-now, and feeling-perceiving-acting are the consistent focus of the work. The unconscious was replaced by the concept of *at-this-moment-unaware*, which refers to the functioning awareness in the here-and-now, bringing the present, rather than the past, on the foreground. This movement does not exclude, though, the inclusion of the past with all its remembering and imagining.

- Wilhelm Reich: F. Perls was in analysis with Reich, and he was clearly influenced by his concept of the *sensing body* as a means of achieving psychological integration and releasing free energy. Unresolved emotional conflicts are believed to be the instigators of chronic character disturbances, manifested in musculo-skeletal armours (see the section on Body psychotherapy in Chapter 6 for more information).
- Gestalt psychologists and especially Kurt Lewin: according to these ancestors, a person perceives and thinks things in organised wholes and coherent patterns (*gestalts*) and not as unrelated isolates. Similarly, psychological relationships are viewed in connection to the surrounding field as no individual can be seen outside their environmental field (see 'field theory' next).
- Holism – Jan Smuts: when F. Perls lived and worked in South Africa he became influenced by the then-prime minister, Smuts, and his concept of 'holism', a radical acceptance of mind–body unity, where inclusion and diversity are seen interconnected and push back the tendency for reductionism of the whole into parts.
- Creative indifference – Salomo Friedlaender: Friedlaender's work on the essential quality of thinking in opposites and his idea of creative indifference as the epitomy of self, absoluteness, will, and freedom inspired F. Perls to conceptualise that fertile void where one's poles of interest are balanced.
- *Self-actualisation* and *organismic self-regulation* – Kurt Goldstein: Laura and Fritz Perls both worked for Goldstein's Institute and were influenced by these two terms that he first coined (see also section on Maslow). As we will see later, the idea of the self as the main motivator for action and for claiming one's potential played an important role in the final synthesis of their theory.
- Phenomenology and existentialism: these two philosophical schools became the major foundations of this approach, and some Gestaltists describe their approach as clinical phenomenology. Edmund Husserl, Jean-Paul Sartre, Maurice Merleau-Merleau-Ponty, and Martin Buber's works are at the heart of the approach that concentrates on the immediate experience and seeks the truth in it by bracketing all assumptions and presuppositions. In Gestalt therapy, clients are enabled to find their own meaning through the process of focusing on the immediate experience; thus, description is considered more important than interpretation. Consciousness is seen as intentional and as intending towards

phenomena, rather than as a free-standing entity. The phenomenological field between the self and the world or the environment
defines the frame of reference for the former.

- Transpersonal elements: Laura Perls's involvement with Eastern
philosophy might be the originator of Buddhist influences in
Gestalt psychotherapy. Enlightenment is achieved through direct,
intuitive experience. Any realisation is achieved through the integration of the rational and the intuitive, together with the actual
experience. The social need for spiritual experience cannot, therefore, be excluded from an approach that sees the self as a whole.
- Creative influences: Fritz was involved in theatre and Laura in
dance and movement. This seems to have given them the basis
from which to integrate creative and experiential techniques in
their approach. It has also been assumed that their technique
of *enactments* has been inspired by Jacob Moreno's psychodrama
(for more information see the section on psychodrama psychotherapy in Chapter 6).

As we can see, Gestalt psychotherapy is an early case of theoretical
integration that stemmed from its founders' restless and curious
minds and from their diverse exposure to theories and experiences in
the world. Over the years, its phenomenological roots have evolved
from awareness of current experience to embracing embodied histories and cognitions to understand experiences (see e.g. the works
of Ruella Frank and Mark Johnson), to actually understanding the
kinaesthetic processes that inform all experiences.

Principles as theory of personality

Since the Gestalt theory of personality evolved from clinical experience, the focus has been on theorising that supports the task of therapists rather than an overall theory of personality and development.
Therefore, I will be choosing the term *principles* to better navigate
you through the main points that shape a therapist's view, assessment
of, and practice with a client.

The starting point is the idea that human beings are in constant
development and movement; they explore, self-reflect, interact in
their social and physical being, whilst they also exist with a certain
element of dependency on their surrounding *field*. The person is

seen holistically and as a complex organism that carries cultural values in all their embodied experiences. The person's body exists as a continuum to the mind, and the person can only exist in relationships. At the same time the theory postulates that people are fundamentally *self-organising* and *self-actualising* beings, who need to make some *creative adjustments* in order to exist.

Equally, psychological disturbance does not happen only because of intra-psychic phenomena, but it's more of a loss of ability to adjust creatively in particular situations. As life flows and change happens, humans are called to continuously extend their adjusting abilities (*freer functioning system*), rather than getting stuck in *fixed gestalts* that limit the self.

The cycle of the formation of self in one's environment starts from the capacity to recognise one's needs. The person creates temporary configurations (*gestalts of a* life) of their experience according to their needs; these dissolve when the experience is completed.

Try to imagine the following sequence of actions in the shape of a circle where each action gives place to the next:

The person is able to sense and feel their dominant need or imbalance → They then allow their feelings and sensations into their awareness → The person mobilises themselves by using physical energy → So, this makes them ready to take action → They are then fully engaged in what they need to do → And they reach a high point of engagement and contact with themselves and the environment → After this intensity the person takes in fully and integrates what happened → And can now let go as this is the end of the cycle of this gestalt → So they return to equilibrium.

There can be, though, some interrupted gestalts that then create unfulfilled states of being. The cause of those interruptions can be environmental, or due to fixed assumptions, or because of lack of awareness, or even consciously chosen. But whatever the reason, they cause a rupture in the *relational field* and even a sense of a *false self*. This is when we can imagine a situation when a person is deep into their trauma or has lost their feeling of security. They react in a certain way which, without support, can cause a frozen and unresolved gestalt. The future development of this gestalt is that it re-emerges when certain associations are made and the person can no longer respond to the actual circumstances of the here-and-now experience; instead, they project the past into the present and they respond with their old patterns. For Gestalt psychotherapy, psychological disturbance can only be deconstructed if lived in the present and also changed in the present. In a way, through therapy, the person becomes aware of their automatic patterns of thinking, feeling, and acting, and the aim is to recognise their alternative choices that can be more life-enhancing and creative.

As we can see so far, there is a cyclical and continuous movement in the way a Gestalt therapist would see their client's functioning in life. At the same time, we have been exploring the ongoing connection to the person's surroundings and circumstances. This is why in Gestalt therapy the client's contact styles give much information about their way of being in the world. There are four kinds of transaction at the *contact boundary*:

(1) How is the contact boundary subjected to overload or potential invasion from the outside? → through introjection, rejection, or creative adjustment
(2) How are feeling expressions, responses, or energy contained? → with adaptability, holding in/back (*retroflection*), or full expression irrespective of the circumstances
(3) How (much) is 'what belongs to self' inaccurately projected onto the environment?
(4) How much does the contact boundary separate self from other? → confluent, extreme differentiation/isolation, or a flexible oscillation between the two

Ideally the person becomes aware of their active participation in their experiences and their several relational fields, builds up their self-support mechanisms, integrates the different disparate parts of themselves, and is able to interact authentically in life.

Practice, ways of being, and techniques

In Gestalt practice the therapist adopts a way of being informed by the principles of the here-and-now, the phenomenological field, processing, contacting, and change. The client is seen in their socio-cultural context and in their matrix of needs.

Although the client's past is important, the therapist focuses in the here-and-now, in the shared experience, and describes what is observed – rather than making interpretations.

The rule of bracketing any biases, assumptions, and expectations and the rule of description allow the therapist to pay attention to what unfolds in their presence and to collect as much information as possible. Furthermore, the rule of equalisation informs the therapist's view on all observed data; they are all of equal importance and with no certain value or hierarchy.

The initial idea that stemmed from Gestalt psychology was that work takes place within the perceptual phenomena. This then evolved into considering the figure and background that continuously reconfigure themselves in the field as part of the process of change. A very classic example is that of the next image; the vase becomes two profiles and vice versa, according to the individual's momentary perception.

Individual momentary perception: vase or two profiles?

Apart from the individual perception, a Gestalt therapist works and attends to the *relational field*. This emerges where subjectivities interact in the immediacy of the moment. The field is the space where the potential for change is explored and, in therapy, encouraged. The two subjects in the field co-influence each other's moment-to-moment subjectivity, experience, and expression. This in-between relational space is, of course, charged by the two subjects' embodied histories and has the potential to regulate them.

Therapist and client meet at a place that is at once physical, phenomenal, and relational, and they both carry their embodied histories that exist outside the context of therapy. They both creatively adjust to their meeting and assimilate or reject elements of it. This way of meeting is called *contacting*. The term highlights that the meeting is a process rather than a static event. The relationship between therapist and client is, thus, referred to as a dialogical one.

This is a rough sequence of the process for meaning-making in therapy:

- The therapist follows the emerging experience of the client→ Then they engage the client through dialogue→ They strategically address aspects of the field→ Finally, they negotiate an experiment with the aim of awareness and learning. The processing of feelings is, therefore, basic to change. The practice of experimenting can take many forms:

- *Enactment* as a move to action: this is when implicit life patterns are experienced in an embodied way within the therapeutic process. The client is asked to put feelings or thoughts into action – either by employing words, saying what they would like to say to the person involved but not present or via role playing. It is a form of awareness raising – rather than catharsis – and allows both therapist and client to connect to that which cannot be verbalised yet.

- *Exaggeration*: this is a special form of enactment and as the word suggests, it acts as a magnifier so that the person can feel the more intense enacted vision.

- *The two-chair method*: still a form of enactment, this method of dialogical experimenting is used to expand and reconfigure two conflicting parts of the self and allows for a more integrated functioning of the self. The client sits on either chair for each part of their self they are exploring.

- *The empty-chair method*: when there is unfinished business in the form of 'unclosed gestalts', a dialogue can be facilitated so that a more dynamic relation between figure and ground can be enabled.

- *Guided fantasy*: this is an alternative to enactment. The client can be given the option of bringing an experience into the here-and-now by visualising.

- *Body techniques*: here we include techniques that facilitate the client's awareness of their body functioning, their embodied history, and stuckness (e.g. the work of Ruella Frank) or techniques that support the expression of certain feelings with the consequent awareness and contact that this can bring.
- *Focusing* (see Gendlin's approach within the PCA): this is a wide range of questions and prompts that encourage the connection, experience, and deepening of certain or unaccessed feelings. For example the therapist might simply ask the client, 'What are you feeling right now?' and they may then prompt them to 'Stay with the feeling'.

The *paradoxical theory of change* is fundamental in Gestalt therapy and its existential experimentalist roots. Very briefly, this refers to the paradox that change can only happen if one trusts their authentic self in the present to lead the way to change rather than putting efforts to make change happen. And this applies to the therapeutic relationship too where neither therapist nor client can coerce change.

A theoretical journey that has led to a relational revision

Gestalt therapy has evolved from its growth-oriented tradition and its socio-cultural focus to a softer, relational, and more dialogic form which is defined as *relational Gestalt therapy*. Gary Yontef, Erving and Miriam Polster (the New York group of Gestaltists) have influenced the more accepting and less confrontational relational turn in the approach. As the most recent development within the approach, it emphasises a shift in the therapist's presence and focus: respect, compassion, acceptance, manifestation of the maximum trust in the process of contact (i.e. the paradoxical theory of change is more prominent in practice), and overall an honest and at the same time empathic process that is attentive to shame-triggering.

Experimentation is still present, but it is used in a more relational manner, with dialogue and deeper awareness of the client, with all their strengths and weaknesses. The therapist is also more alert to their impact on the client, thus more attentive to and curious about ruptures in the field.

As with all relational developments in the other approaches we have seen in previous sections of this book, here also it is believed that each relational moment in therapy symbolises something from the client's larger picture of their life. Relational Gestalt psychotherapy has integrated the foundations of Levinas's phenomenological philosophy: the self is defined by their intersubjective relationality and is infused with sensibility. Fellow human-feeling and sensibility inform the therapy practice too.

EXISTENTIAL PSYCHOTHERAPY: WHEN PHILOSOPHY MEETS PSYCHOTHERAPY

Existential therapy is a philosophically informed approach that incorporates a diverse spectrum of theories and practices. Because of its evolving diversity, it is hard to define a particular way of being for existential therapists. Nevertheless, there are some fundamental principles that navigate all existential therapists:

- People are seen as always in relation and never in isolation. An individual lives, functions, relates, and grows in a world, with people and in certain situations.
- Therefore, any problems need to be seen in their socio-political and cultural context.
- Therapy helps people to come to terms with life, its ongoing complexity, and the paradoxes of their everyday existence. The problems people bring to therapy are the result of their inner struggle with the challenges and limitations of the human condition.
- The concept of self is relative and in constant transformation, and the capacity for understanding it depends on the capacity to face the truth and aim for authenticity in relation to others.

From these principles we can see why existential therapy is a humanistic approach, despite some ongoing debates about it.

The roots of the approach

Existential therapy has its roots in existential philosophy that tried to make sense of human existence, and its predominant method, phenomenology. We can trace back its influencers in the 19th century with philosophers such as Arthur Schopenhauer, Kierkegaard, and Friedrich Nietzsche, and then in the 20th century with Martin Heidegger and Husserl as the main pillars of the approach. There is, of course, the influence by the 20th-century French existentialists (see Sartre, Simone de Beauvoir, Albert Camus, and Merleau-Ponty) and the European existentially oriented philosophers such as Michel Foucault, Levinas, Jacques Derrida, Buber, Max Scheler, Paul Tillich, and Hannah Arendt.

The following are some foundational ideas that are relevant to existential psychotherapy:

- Husserl: his theory was based on the experience of the human world as one's scientific foundation. He coined the term *bracketing* which refers to the conscious process of reduction of the natural world and its interpretation in order to observe the actual phenomenon in front of us.

- Heidegger: his work evolved around the question of what is meant by the verb 'to be'. *Dasein* (*being-in-the-world*) is seen as one's inherent need to exist in the world, as a single entity where self and world belong together. Being is also interlinked with time and all these give us the sense that there is no fixed existence, but we are always 'becoming'. This sharing of our world with others gives us some understanding of both our own selves and others (see empathy). In people's constant projection of themselves into the future, we can see at the same time the emergence of the 'becoming' from their past. Finally, guilt is a feeling that emerges due to one's being torn between authentic and inauthentic modes of living; the latter being the result of facing up to the human condition and the choices within the timeline of past-present-future.

- Sartre: he saw people as condemned to be free, and at the same time he spoke about the exaggeration of existential anxiety of consciousness in the face of *bad faith*; people's refusal to take responsibility for their choices and the consequent conforming to given roles and social attributions. Shame for Sartre is the result of *the look*, where the person is then objectified and they see themselves as such. At the same time he believes that reflective consciousness arises through the relationship with others.

- Merleau-Ponty: he replaced Heidegger's *being-in-the-world* with *flesh-in-the-world*, theorising in this way our bodies from a phenomenological perspective. Consciousness for Merleau-Ponty is practical, perceptual, and embodied; we *are* our bodies, we don't simply possess our bodies. Our bodies are the vehicles of being in the world, and we can see them as subjective (i.e. the lived experience) and objective (i.e. as observed and investigated by scientists but also as known by the Other who can objectify one's body).

- De Beauvoir: she postulated that women are seen as the Other in our patriarchal societies and spearheaded the white Western feminist movement. For de Beauvoir 'one is not born a woman', she's made into one when we consider existence preceding essence. She also spoke about the tyranny of power and the human responsibility to fight back in order to maintain the *truth* of our freedom.

- Buber: he is known for his work on the potential of the 'I–Thou relationship' with all its mutuality, absence of judgement, openness to and acceptance of the Other, and the authenticity that comes from the valuing of the Other and the consequent mutual sharing (see also his influence on Carl Rogers). For Buber any communication has the potential of a reciprocal exchange and openness to awareness and it's not just a conversation. He also highlighted the *between* in the communication, rather than just the individual offering or even the offering that comes together from the people involved.

- Levinas: his philosophy of ethics prioritises the Other and the concern for them. For Levinas there will always be some asymmetry in the relationship of self–Other, as the Other is an eternal stranger and the self cannot experience the Other as if they were the latter. His view of humans is as complacent to societal narratives, self-absorbed, and inauthentic and attributes to the Other a wake-up call and a reminder of individual responsibility and potential for goodness.

It is beyond the scope of this introductory book to go into more detail on each of the theories that these important philosophers have gifted to the Western world, so for information please see the suggested references at the end of this section.

The main themes around which all the previously mentioned philosophers tried to understand human existence are destiny, anxiety (*Angst*) and its avoidance, choice, responsibility, despair, fate, individuality and subjectivity, power, and the overall meaning of being.

Do the previously mentioned themes sound familiar to you when it comes to thinking about reaching out for therapy?

How often do you consider the ideas of one's lived experience and truth of our freedom or the process of becoming?

The formation of the four existential schools of thought

Some philosophically oriented psychiatrists, psychologists, and psychoanalysts adopted these philosophical theories and created the following existential schools:

(1) Daseinsanalysis (analysis of being-there) or existential analysis

The first person to attempt to describe the experience of people with mental health problems without labelling the individuals by imposing diagnoses was the German psychiatrist Karl Jaspers. Jaspers tried to understand the individual and make sense of their experience in existential terms. He also tried to explore the idea that one can become what their potential is only by exploring their natural limits.

Parallelly in Switzerland, Ludwig Binswanger was introducing phenomenology into psychiatry by bringing existential reflections into his work in sanatoriums. He practised with the perspective that therapy ought to focus on helping people to rediscover their spirit and desire for life. His student, Medard Boss, took this work further by articulating a phenomenological approach to psychoanalysis.

Binswanger introduced Boss to Heidegger's work, and together they are seen as the founders of this approach that combines psychoanalysis with Heidegger's fundamental ontology.

(2) Logotherapy and therapies of meaning

Viktor Frankl's theory about meaning as the central motivational force for humans shaped his psychotherapeutic approach, *logotherapy*, as well as later contemporary therapies of meaning.

Frankl believed in existential therapy as a means of helping clients (re) discover – rather than internally create – purpose and meaning in their lives and in relation to the world they live in, and he applied his theory in his seminal book *Man's Search for Meaning* that described his three-year experience as a Jewish man in four concentration camps during the Second World War. He also saw the centrality of the vacuum of meaning in people's life in the modern world, in relation to mental health.

Further to logotherapy, there are also other *therapies of meaning* that have their roots in logotherapy but also integrate other approaches and techniques (e.g. *meaning-centred* therapy). The umbrella of logotherapy and meaning therapies are more directive and focused compared to the other existential therapy approaches, and they include a wide range of techniques.

(3)   The new European movement

In the '60s and '70s, there was a turn into an existential phenomenological approach in therapy, mainly in the UK. Starting with R.D. Laing's inspirational work in therapeutic communities and the challenge to status quo (see *anti-psychiatry movement*), therapy is seen as a form of anti-establishment. Laing was influenced by the later existential philosophies of Sartre, etc. Psychotic symptoms were understood by philosophical concepts rather than medical ones, the term 'madness' was seen as a label used by those who were inconvenienced by the individuals who were trying to express themselves in an attempt to escape the double-bindness of society and family, and mental health problems (especially schizophrenia) were seen as part of both a personal and a social struggle. For Laing and his followers, any kind of expression that is within the psychotic spectrum needs to be considered within the family and political context within which the individual was born and exists. Also, there was the belief that a breakdown could lead to a breakthrough.

A different revival of existential therapy in the UK started in the '80s and continues today with Emmy van Deurzen and Ernesto Spinelli, and later by their followers. Van Deurzen's school of theory and practice is based on the aim to help clients to realise any self-deceptions or alienation caused by their resistance to face the challenging existences they live, as well as to discover and pursue their potential and possibilities.

Spinelli's approach, on the other hand, is perceived as more relational and with an emphasis on the importance of the unknown. The therapist is in a continuous process of bracketing their beliefs and assumptions, and they relate to their clients from a stance of un-knowing.

Both these developments, though, have engaged with the problems of living rather than mental health.

(4) Existential-humanistic and existential-integrative therapy

Existential-humanistic therapy originated in the USA, and it tried to blend ideas from the European existential philosophy and psychotherapy that we encountered earlier in this section, alongside the American perspective of humanistic psychology.

Rollo May is perceived as the founder of the approach, and it was him who tried to bridge interpersonal psychoanalysis (see Sullivan's work in Chapter 2) with European existentialism and phenomenology (more specifically the work of Binswanger and Boss). His 1958 seminal book *Existence*, alongside Henri Ellenberger and Ernest Angel, influenced the whole 'human potential movement' of that time.

May's primary attention was on freedom and destiny. He saw the dynamic polarities of these two concepts as a meaning for life source, and freedom as a responsibility and a capacity to choose within life's many limitations.

May's contemporary and also one of the founders of humanistic psychology, James Bugental, placed emphasis on the self as embodied and saw this as ever-changing. For Bugental, the individual exists in the extremes of choice and restriction, isolation and relation, and they need to face any change by sorting through the different layers involved and coming out of this process with a meaningful and action-oriented response. His work also focused on the concept of therapeutic presence, how this is applied in practice and how this is also translated into an authentic and responsible life.

Later, Irvin Yalom popularised the approach and highlighted the importance of the therapeutic relationship, postulating that change and growth can only happen within a safe and intimate therapeutic relationship. His work is influenced by Buber's values on the 'I–Thou relationship'. Yalom also bases his work on the *four givens* of human existence: death, freedom, isolation, and meaninglessness. So, a client has to face the challenge of confronting these *givens* and prioritising their mechanisms to integrate, explore, and co-exist with these *givens*.

In the '90s, Kirk Schneider and Rollo May suggested the development of existential-integrative therapy that embraces diverse levels of client contact as well as diverse interventions from several psychological models (see nonexperiential-medical and behavioural, to experiential-existential and transpersonal), and embraces Yalom's idea that a new therapy is created with each client. It is an approach that pays tribute to both the constrictive and expansive capacities and encourages responses to these and an ability to integrate the latter into a dynamic whole.

General foundations

As we can see from the different schools and the different philosophical influences, there is no one theory of personality in existential psychotherapy, but there is some consensus on certain principles:

- The origin of problems is one's escape from reality and into an illusion when it comes to difficulties, giving away in this manner one's freedom and the responsibility of making their own choices and changes in life. The extreme of this is when people isolate from the world or find themselves in a state of severe psychopathology.
- Change is seen as a continuous way of being, but equally existential psychotherapy acknowledges people's need for stability. Therefore, an existential psychotherapist seeks to enable clients to build up their awareness and tolerance of their anxieties and to be open to the fluidity and paradox of their lives. Any crisis is seen as both a danger and an opportunity for reorganisation and transformation.
- Freedom is a fundamental quality on personality and life shaping. But freedom is not just about autonomy, it is mainly about the choices one makes at a certain point, which then shape one's future encounters.
- Thus, for existential psychotherapy the self is not determined but fluid and dynamic. The self is in a continuous state of becoming despite the fear and anxiety that this unstable process might have.
- Humans exist in relations; therefore, a client is seen and supported in their intersubjective network and histories.
- The past and the future exist in one's present experience and are seen as ground and meaning to understand the lived time. Therefore, one's temporality is significant in the choices they make in the present.
- Existential anxiety and guilt are not seen as symptoms but as signals that give information about one's resistance or avoidance to face the *givens of existence* (meaninglessness, responsibility, isolation, freedom, and death) and the responsibility that these require.

- Being true to one's experience of the world (including openness to the world, the other's and one's own experience) and confronting the *givens of existence* shape one's authenticity.

Overall, existential psychotherapy is a fundamentally relational approach that sees the therapeutic relationship and the therapist's presence as the main corrective experiences. No techniques are used as they can dilute the deep human experiences and interactions in therapy, but some conversational strategies might be employed. Equally, psychopathology labels are seen as obstructive to the processes of meaning-making and embodiment of authenticity.

TRANSACTIONAL ANALYSIS (TA): EGO STATES IN TRANSACTIONS AND IN GAMES

In the '50s, a Canadian-American psychiatrist and psychoanalyst, Eric Berne, made an original contribution by creating a multifaceted theory that integrated the classical psychoanalytic notion of intra-psychic dynamics with the humanistic principle of interpersonal behaviours. The interactional emphasis of his approach is captured in the term used to name it, *transactional*. The inclusion of TA in the humanistic family becomes more obvious when we consider (1) its main philosophical point that human beings strive towards health and can reach their full potential if they are given the right opportunities, (2) its egalitarian and co-responsible understanding of the therapeutic relationship and the respect of the client's subjectivity, (3) its influence from phenomenology and Berne's vision of TA as a *systematic phenomenology*, and (4) Berne's view of the therapist's social responsibility.

In terms of theoretical influences, Berne initially shaped his own theory based on Freud's and Skinner's theories. Later there were influences from object relations theory and strong influences from cognitive behaviourism.

TA became very popular after the publication of Berne's book *Games People Play* in the mid-'60s. Even today, in our everyday vocabulary, we use some of his concepts in expressions such as 'the child in that person' or 'they play psychological games'. The simplicity of the language and terminology have also contributed to TA's popularity, given the complex language of psychoanalysis that nurtured an elitist climate around psychotherapy.

The central thread of TA runs through three basic philosophical points and the principles that support them:

Philosophical points

- People are OK: this is a point that highlights everyone's equal value and worth as human beings. It's our accounting for 'we-ness' and 'I-ness' at the same time, a process of becoming conscious of ourselves, therefore leading to genuine congruent relationships in a healthy adult functioning mode.
- People can think: human beings can think about and evaluate their experiences. This point is where we can see TA's valuing of people as it promotes their resources and well-being.
- People and their decisions can change: as a theory with much investment in hope, TA's belief is in people's capacity to think; therefore, they can decide their own destiny in their context and can change their decisions.

Principles

- Open communication: clear and transparent communication and simple language are essential contributions from the therapist for the client to play an equal part in the relationship and to feel empowered in their process for change.
- Contractual method: the client's agreement is of the highest importance throughout the whole therapy process. From the initial stage of the contract to the decision for termination, the seeking for the client's agreement supports the equality in the therapeutic relationship, highlights the joint responsibility of the therapy process, and keeps a vigilant eye on the potential power imbalance.
- Above all, do no harm: an appropriate, thoughtful, and sensitive use of the therapist's skills and knowledge is necessary to avoid any harm caused by the power of the therapist's role.

Image of the person and personality development

OK positions and drives

The fundamental worth of people, as a basic concept in Berne's original theory, is called *OK-ness*. It is not just about approving people's behaviours but mainly respecting and valuing people and what they bring in relationships.

One is born with the basic drive for health and growth and a need for loving recognition (*OK*). In the interactions over one's lifetime there can be the following variations of OK between the individual and the other/context: 'I'm OK-You're not OK', 'I'm not OK-You're OK', 'I'm not OK-You're not OK'. The desired position despite all the existential obstacles is the 'I'm ok-You're OK' one where the individual in relationship can reach their full potential and self-actualise.

In all the previously mentioned interpersonal processes of OK-ness, Berne postulates that three drives exist: the death instinct (*mortido*), the sexual instinct (*libido*), and a general and eternal creative force towards growth (*physis*). The first two drives stem from Freud's theory and his Thanatos and Eros ideas. The latter is an important addition to any theory of drives as it recognises the nurturing role and creative force of nature where growth is encouraged and progress comes through an order of events. In TA theory there is a belief in the drives as corrective elements in any hereditary limitations (e.g. learning difficulties or physical disabilities); the drive towards psychological health can overcome or modify those limitations.

Ego states or ways of being during interactions

Berne elaborated the psychoanalytic idea of ego states and created a theory of therapy to directly influence and change those states (see further in this section). Ego states have been described as 'chunks of psychic time', and they are the subjectively experienced realities of a person's mind–body ego with the original contents of the time period they represent. Each ego state is an entire system of thoughts, feelings, and behaviours from which an individual interacts with others.

The idea of ego states is based on psychoanalytic theory in which childhood experiences and parenting patterns affect our lives as adults and contribute to the formation of the three ego states.

A *child ego state* is a multitude of states (e.g. the adapted or the free child ego state) which represent one's earlier developmental history and are accessible to being relived in the present – reverting into the thinking and feeling processes of our childhood.

A *parent ego state* is the thinking and behaving that has been internalised by one's parents or important authority figures and is represented in the way the person relates to others and to themselves. It is a reactive state that stems from one's conditioning and how they have copied their parents' behaviours in similar situations, without questioning them in the here-and-now.

An *adult ego state* represents the biologically mature person who is conscious of their emotional world, has developed and holds particular beliefs and values, and is able to think clearly and cope effectively with any needs that are present in the here-and-now. Autonomy is the dominant quality – versus dependence and conditioning that characterise the two previous ego states.

Interactions from either the child or the parent ego states are unconscious and demonstrate themselves as default reactions; on the other hand, when conscious awareness is present, the individual can bring themselves back into an adult ego state and interact from that place instead. The aim of therapy, therefore, is to reach a multiple state of consciousness under the direction of an integrated adult ego state.

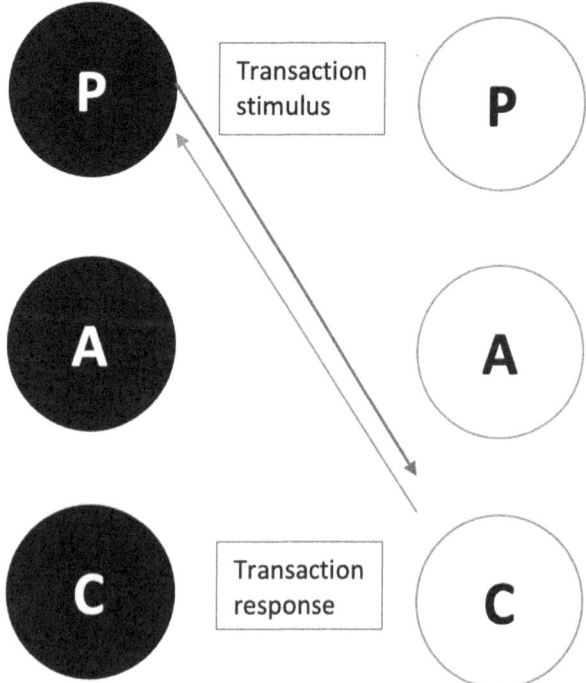

Transaction stimuli and responses amongst the ego states

Scripting, psychological disturbance, and dysfunctional behaviours

Scripting is a psychological and cognitive process of concluding and decision making that starts from early childhood as a response to survival in particular circumstances. It's a sense-making process based on early experiences and interactions. *Scripts*, therefore, are all those unconsciously built beliefs and views about one's self, others, and the world, formed out of the child's response to their environment and their interactions with their parents and important adults.

Scripting, though, limits one's capacity for awareness, emotional proximity, or spontaneity as survival becomes the main focus. Since scripts are decisions that impact one's life from childhood to adulthood, they are responsible for psychological disturbance and dysfunctional behaviours. Psychological disturbance can also occur in adulthood due to trauma or psychological strain, and TA looks at it in three different ways:

- Confusion model: here the functioning of the integrated adult ego is impeded by the *contamination* that occurs when either the parent ego state intrudes (e.g. prejudices) or the child ego state intrudes (e.g. phobias). Limiting beliefs, traumatic experiences, and/or learnt emotional and physiological response become the obstacles for conscious awareness of the here-and-now.
- Conflict model: psychological disturbance is seen here as internal stuck points between the different ego states. It's a state of deadlock that requires resolution for the personality to develop and for the needs, feelings, and values to be expressed and pursued.
- Developmental deficit and inadequate parenting model: inadequate, abusive, or neglectful parenting during the formative years of a child results in psychological disturbances.

Berne also observed that people need *strokes*, the gestures of vitally needed interpersonal recognition for a child to survive and thrive. Therefore, scripting is also affected by the giving or withholding of strokes. Psychological disturbance is perpetuated when one seeks out the same strokes and same stroking patterns that became habitual in their childhood.

Transactions are the communication exchanges between people, the smallest units of the stimulus–response process that are then recreated in life. Berne defined three categories of transactions that either further or perpetuate the script and consequently support or hinder communications: *complementary* (predictable), *crossed* (unpredictable), and *ulterior* (with hidden agenda). *Games* are a series of repetitive transactions with a socially dysfunctional nature. Their principal intention is to obtain strokes, but instead they reinforce negative self-concepts and create obstacles to direct and sincere emotional and thought expression. Games are played out outside the adult ego state and have the power of repetition and predictability.

Theory of therapy

Berne was a great advocate of the equality and trust required to build a therapeutic relationship. He postulated that it requires a specific treatment plan and diagnosis, held within a clear theoretical framework. In other words, it can't just happen. The emphasis of TA is on the acceptance and valuing of the client as necessary foundations, as well as an expectation that both therapist and client are responsible for their own response and behaviour in the field between them. Through the multilayered creation that happens in the therapeutic relationship, the clients' life project for evolution is constantly encouraged and empowered. The therapy experience allows the individual to configure their sense of self, of other, and of life in general.

At the heart of TA is the diagnosis of ego states with four different but complementary methods to do so: (1) *behavioural diagnosis* that is based on what is observed there-and-then, (2) *social diagnosis* made by witnessing the reactions other people have towards the client and as response to their behaviour, (3) *historical diagnosis* that validates historically a past experience, and (4) *phenomenological diagnosis* based on subjective self-examination.

The initial stages of therapy involve a process of parent or child *decontamination* of the adult ego state (*confusion model*) and aim for a fully integrated adult ego state, without the interference of unresolved experiences. Later, the work is focused on clarifying and resolving any stuckness (*conflict model*), and it culminates in a reparative process to meet the unmet developmental needs (*deficit model*) that can lead to a healthy sense of self (e.g. mirroring).

Another layer of reparation is through the therapist's understanding of the client's stroke giving and receiving process. *Script analysis* allows for exploration of childhood scripts, of any positive or negative reinforcements that have built up over the years, and of all the subtle messages received in the form of *injunctions*. Changing the *life script* is the aim in TA therapy, and it means that any unhelpful or unhealthy scripting is replaced with more cooperative and congruent behaviours. In script analysis, the therapist facilitates the *games analysis* in which the focus is on the identification of the dysfunctional transactions so that these are processed and space is made for furthering the script.

Physis (nature in Greek) as a driving force is manifested through change, from psychological disturbance to health. This process, consequently, leads towards *autonomy*. In TA, autonomy is composed of three qualities: awareness, spontaneity, and intimacy. Autonomy as a goal of therapy supports consciousness, the valuing of expression, and satisfying interpersonal relationships. If we saw autonomy as script release, we can also see why another goal of TA therapy is symptom relief, and if a person chooses to embark on an in-depth therapy journey, they then aim for script cure too.

Levels of therapy

Contractual therapeutic relationship (the I'm OK–You're OK position) is the foundation of TA therapy. The client is encouraged to be involved in the goal setting and planning of therapy and to take an active role in their own understanding of therapy and their process. Then the relationship evolves into a *transferential* one with the externalisation of previous intra-psychic relationships onto the therapist. The next stage is that of a *reparative/developmentally needed* relationship where all the script and games analysis happen. The *core relationship* draws the two (therapist and client) integrated adult egos together making genuine encounters possible. Finally, the ultimate level of relating in TA therapy is called *transpersonal relationship* and depicts the relationship of both therapist and client to physis.

Therapeutic interventions

I will name here some TA therapeutic strategies and techniques that are used as interventions. The range is wide as it covers both a practical element in a therapist's work and certain relational ways of being (some of the terms are explained earlier and I will not be explaining them again due to space limitations):

- Contracting: treatment contracts are integral in TA therapy and emphasise the client's responsibility for their own treatment, maximise cooperation, and allow for observable outcomes that have been set as goals
- Decontamination
- Stuckness resolution (conflict model)
- Parenting and reparenting (deficit model)
- Interrogation, specification, confrontation, and explanation
- Illustration, confirmation, interpretation, and crystallisation
- Enquiry, empathy, attunement, and involvement

The expansion of the classical school

Berne's initial theory and therapy model has been expanded since his death in 1970, and there are now several branches within the international community of TA therapists:

- *Cathexis school*: this is the creation of the Cathexis Institute and Jacqui Schiff and her colleagues who were working with clients with psychosis. It is the TA branch that focused on the technique of 'reparenting'. For this school, poor parenting in childhood constitutes the core of many here-and-now problems in adulthood.
- *Redecision school*: Robert and Mary Goulding integrated TA and Gestalt theories and practices and created the following sequence of events in clients' development: one's earliest decisions are stored in their psyche as feelings rather than as thoughts–decisions —> it is necessary for the client to access those early feelings and then express them so that they can make a new appropriate *redecision* —> the client's feeling, thinking, and behaving processes are now different.
- *Integrative movement*: this is the movement led by Barbara Clark, Petruska Clarkson, and Richard Erskine where they integrated TA with self psychology and the latter's emphasis on the importance of empathy and attunement.

- *Co-creative TA*: Keith Tudor has tried to bring together the psychodynamic, political, and person-centered perspectives with TA and to emphasise the process of mutual conscious and unconscious influence in the therapeutic relationship.
- *Context TA*: this is Karen Minikin's attempt to bring TA back to its socio-political roots with the preoccupations, biases, and concerns of our time and the consequent psychological and social responses.
- *Contemporary TA*: the most recent development, this is where TA re-meets psychoanalysis but in its relational form. This is a branch that focuses on the client's and therapist's subjectivity and any unconscious relating, with special focus on transference and countertransference.

AS THE FAMILY EXPANDED

TRANSPERSONAL PSYCHOTHERAPY: THE SPIRITUAL AND SOUL AS PARTS OF THERAPY

Transpersonal psychology was Maslow's and Sutich's creation after their dissatisfaction with the spiritual being left out of the experiential and social transformations of the '60s. It was a countercultural movement aligned with the intense social and relational changes of that time, namely: (1) multiculturalism and its consequent exposure to non-Western spiritual traditions (e.g. meditation), (2) psychedelic experimentation with the pushback for imposed realities, and (3) social justice with all the authority questioning that led to the protests for civil rights or against the imperialistic and even against scientific claims and practices that served the political elite and status quo.

So, Maslow and Sutich founded the *Journal of Transpersonal Psychology* in 1969 – and later on the Association for Transpersonal Psychology within the American Psychological Association – and not only reintroduced the spiritual dimension back to psychotherapy, but also highlighted the importance of a paradigm shift from a human-centred psychology to a cosmos-centered one. Transpersonal psychology then became the fourth force of Western psychology. Despite this shift, I – as well as many other writers – choose to include it within the humanistic theories umbrella as it shares the values I mentioned in this chapter's introduction, and it was created within humanistic circles.

This is a therapy approach that draws from both Western and Eastern world views. What made a difference in the initial stages was the stance of learning from traditions that were underestimated before and furthering them through scientific methods. Therefore, we can see transpersonal psychology as a crucible in which the wisdom of the two world views, spiritual traditions, and practices can integrate in an attempt to answer the perpetual question of humankind, 'Who am I?'

The focus shifted to people's spiritual dimensions of experience, meditation, and metavalues and, mainly, higher states of consciousness for the exploration and facilitation of the actualisation of self and being. Consciousness was divided between 'normal' (i.e. defences that contract the self from their expansion) and 'optimum'. The latter facilitates growth as it involves letting go of the defences, therefore removing those obstacles that get in the way of recognising one's ever-present expanded potential. Similarly, personality was seen as only one aspect of being; one may but does not have to identify with it.

An important innovation that transpersonal psychology made was the emphasis it put on the extension of the sense of self beyond the individual (see the meaning of 'trans-'), beyond the personal. Wider aspects of humankind and life, cosmos, psyche, and the other-than-human were encompassed in the pursuit of a whole sense of self. This is what extreme interconnectedness meant in practice. It also highlights and facilitates the expression of the spiritual in and through the personal and also the transcendence of the self.

In the therapy and psychology fields that struggled to prove everything scientifically in a narrow empirical way, transpersonal psychology came to reiterate the importance of subjective experience. Under the umbrella of subjective experience this theory has focused on the realisation of ultimate states and the fluidity between the conscious and the unconscious. For transpersonal theorists the self/soul/psyche is in a consistently active striving for health, meaning, and wholeness, and the primary aim is towards a more mindful awareness of experiences and not so much towards the change of experiences. Some expressions that represent this process in transpersonal literature are individuation, awakening, enhanced awareness, and liberation.

Here I feel compelled to clarify how even Maslow felt it was necessary to distinguish between spirituality and religion. The potential confusion of these two terms has created obstacles in making this approach more widely accepted. Maslow referred to institutional religion as the 'big R' religion and to personal spirituality as the 'little R' religion. We can see religion as all those organised and established structures that facilitate organised religion and provide meaning to some people, whilst spirituality is connected to the soul's free and ongoing quest for peak experiences and the connection with the divine; and it's not necessarily connected to an organised religion.

We can trace back the roots of the spirituality dimension in William James's work, the 'father of American psychology' in the 19th century. James perceived one's soul as existing in a spiritual universe, and his theories were influenced by spiritualism, a school of thought by itself.

Furthermore, we cannot ignore the substantial influence Jung's theories had on many transpersonal theorists, and therefore, he can be perceived as the grandfather of the approach (for more information on his theory on spirituality, see Chapter 2). In the '70s his work was taken a step further by James Hillman who popularised the idea of the power of the soul and its connection to mythological imagery that belongs to the collective unconscious.

Another predecessor to the transpersonalists was Roberto Assagioli and his own school of *psychosynthesis*. Psychosynthesis is based on Freud's idea of the unconscious and his notion of the inner and interpersonal conflict, but it also addresses the life journey of the individual; a journey towards self-realisation, peak experiences, spiritual insight, and higher states of consciousness. Assagioli believed in the superconscious or transpersonal self, with the aim of the 'I' aligning itself with it. His work explains how initially the individual identifies with what is in the lower unconscious and its various *subpersonalities*. Gradually and through compassionate attention and by looking beyond those identifications, the individual disidentifies from those lower contents and this is where they get in touch with their higher unconscious or transpersonal self, with all the deeper knowledge of the self that this achieves. That more integral part of the self encompasses both the uniquely personal and the transpersonal as a demonstration of the human impulse towards wholeness. Psychosynthesis pioneered the work of guided imagery and recognised through this the *inner child*, a term now widely used by other theories too.

> What role do non-Western spiritual traditions play in your everyday life, and if any do you see this in the wholeness of mind–body–spirit?
>   Have you felt that a spiritual dimension is necessary in your journey towards reaching your potential?
>   Is the concept of the inner child helpful when you try to understand yourself as an adult in today's world?

Because transpersonal psychotherapy encompasses many viewpoints that are not connected through a central theory of personality and development – in contrast to the other theories we have seen so far – but more by certain assumptions and values, there is no unified and clearly defined approach but several schools of thought and practice. I will describe here the two most influential models by Ken Wilber and Stanislav Grof.

Up until Wilber's seminal book *The Spectrum of Consciousness*, there were very few solid ideas on how spiritual and psychological growth overlap or inform each other. Wilber's work de-stigmatised the consciousness of neurosis or psychosis by demonstrating that the consciousness of mystical states is closely related to it. Also, he postulated that consciousness is composed of many different levels or bands, including the primary levels of the ego, the existential, and the level of mind.

Wilber showed how psychotherapy can become the basis for spiritual development. In his theory all existing theories and philosophies are seen as part of the jigsaw that creates the wisdom for human consciousness. He also highlighted the difference between pre-personal states of consciousness in childhood, where self-consciousness is not yet developed, and transpersonal states, where the individual has gone through self-consciousness and the latter has transcended to the point that the individual is no longer ego-bound but remains self-reflexive.

Wilber's spectrum starts with psychosis as the fragmented and limited consciousness and then continues upward with neurosis and existential levels of consciousness (see Western psychology and psychotherapy theories sitting here). The upper levels of consciousness consist of spiritual systems, and enlightenment is on the level of widest consciousness, the most unified.

Further developments of his spectrum focused on the integration of developmental stages and the reflection of potential developmental arrests as seen in Freud's work, or in the developmental psychologist, Jean Piaget's, work. He named those levels as *prepersonal–personal–transpersonal.*

Grof developed his *holotropic model* by using altered states of consciousness to meet the goals of therapy for his clients. His pioneering work has given proof and respectability to the use of psychedelics in psychotherapy. Through his observations and research he created the map of consciousness with its three broad territories: (1) the realm of the sensory barrier and the personal unconscious, (2) the perinatal/birth-related realm, and (3) the transpersonal realm.

Grof sees the psychological work through the substages of the realms as non-linear, but he does postulate that any work done on each substage leads to resolution and forward movement. He also sees his model and the stages as an integration and movement from Freud's to Reich's and Rank's and finally, to Jung's theories.

His work is based on psychiatry and LSD research, and he also uses holotropic breathwork (e.g. breathing at a fast rate for minutes to hours) and loud music as a substitute for LSD, which at the time of writing remains illegal in many parts of the world. Facilitated in groups, the work is then organised in pairs with one member being the breather and the other the sitter who holds the space and process. At the end of the session the facilitator encourages all group members to draw mandalas of their experience and to share verbally their process as the last step for integration.

Finally, it is important to mention one of the newer developments within the transpersonal family, the *Re-Vision integrative transpersonal model* that brings together Wilber's model alongside with psychodynamic theories – including relational psychoanalysis, attachment theory, and analytical and archetypal psychology – psychosynthesis, Gestalt and other embodied theories and practices, neuroscience, and family systems theory. It is based on a circular view of psychological development and ego formation: pre-cognitive (pre-formation) to cognitive (ego formation) to trans-cognitive (transformation) and back again to pre-cognitive.

Some of the core ideas that have also been evolving this model are the soul, the wounded healer, Eros, and the synergetic/intersubjective field.

.

FEMINIST PSYCHOTHERAPY: WHEN THE PERSONAL IS RECOGNISED AS POLITICAL

With the second wave of feminism sparking in the late '60s, a new therapy approach emerged. Feminist psychotherapy was the child of the Women's Liberation Movement against sexism and misogyny, and it reflected the concerns raised by that movement whilst responding to the challenges and emerging needs of women. Alongside its psychoanalytic sister (see the section on feminist psychoanalysis in Chapter 2), feminist psychotherapy aimed to develop a viable alternative for women who wanted to engage in therapy, without the burdens and obstacles of sexism, misogyny, and stereotyping that have always stigmatised the therapy and mental health fields.

Feminist therapy specialises in gender and how women's emotional health is directly affected by the biases, discrimination, and oppression imposed by systemic patriarchy. The latter is seen as the primary source of human (not only women's) distress, including the distress of diagnostic categories and labelled psychopathology defined by the medical system. Based on feminist ethics of care, this is an approach that started from grassroots activism and is characterised by intersectional commitment and consciousness–raising.

Theoretically speaking, it is an integrative approach but with a political view of therapy; both therapist and client work towards strategies and plans to advance feminist resistance and to transform daily personal, relational, social, and emotional environments as part of the social change aim.

Because of the recognition of the personal being political, it is an approach that privileges and focuses on the voices and experiences of the margins, of those who have been defined as the 'other' by the dominant patriarchal mainstream. In feminist therapy human beings are perceived as responsive to the problems of their lives, as these are caused by certain biased contexts, and at the same time they are seen as capable of solving those problems and striving for change.

As a political approach, it sees the therapeutic relationship and the client's experiences within the framework of societal and cultural realities, and with the dynamics of power that inform those realities.

Therefore, the therapeutic relationship is based on authenticity and equality and the client, as a member of marginalised groups, is considered the source of wisdom. The latter is one more element of practice that opposes the dominant allocation of expertise on the therapist, which stems from patriarchal structures and ideology.

Feminist therapy is based on some core values:

- Consciousness-raising (as the equivalent centre of the psychoanalytic concept of the unconscious): a process of analysing the experienced oppression and the implications of sexism for women's well-being
- Awareness of power dynamics (including within the therapeutic relationship)
- The personal is political
- Mental illness and diagnoses deconstruction and redefining
- Embodied and relational work to access the deeply rooted systemic patriarchy
- Marginalised viewpoints becoming central and intersectional identities being honoured
- Therapy experience can only be situated within the broad social and political contexts informing constructions of gender, power, and powerlessness

As a political movement, there weren't specific founders, but it is worth mentioning some of the pioneers: Jean Miller, with her *relational-cultural theory*; Phyllis Chesler, with her seminal book *Women and Madness* highlighting the double standards between women and men regarding mental health diagnosis and treatment and the punitive societal attitudes against the former; Miriam Greenspan, who incorporated the political and spiritual dimensions of experience; Judith Herman, with her work on abuse and trauma; Reiko Homma-True, who voiced the double oppression off racism and sexism; Lenore Walker, who influenced scientific and cultural views of domestic violence; Carol Gilligan, with her theory on women's relationship-oriented concern for care and connectedness in our dominant androcentric world that celebrates logic and reasoning; and Laura Brown and Oliva Espín, who placed feminist therapy in an international and intersectional context that places multiculturalism at the core of the theory and practice.

Despite the historical association of feminist therapy provided to women by women, today's feminist therapy is open also to people of any gender, to couples, families, or children and is practised by therapists of all genders.

Does feminism form your understanding and embodiment of the world, and if yes, do you remember how and when you became aware of it?

What is your understanding of the personal being political based on your own intersectional identity?

Do you see patriarchy affecting the way therapy is conceptualised and practised?

ENCOUNTER GROUPS AND CO-COUNSELLING: THE RADICAL CHILDREN OF THE GROWTH MOVEMENT ENCOUNTER GROUPS

Whilst all the previously mentioned therapy approaches developed a group therapy version of their initial model, it was the idea of facilitating 'therapy groups for normals' that initiated the development of encounter groups in the '60s and '70s. Encounter groups were seen as part of the then social movement with its focus on growth; therefore, the experience in these groups is perceived not as therapy but as a process of growth and the members are considered participants, not clients. Encounter, after all, means a real meeting between people.

Historically, encounter groups were influenced by Kurt Lewin's '40s *T-groups*. These were research groups with volunteer participants that focused on the study of group dynamics as part of Lewin's field theory. The main concepts were that, given the right conditions, a person will choose growth and positive interactions – rather than the opposite qualities – and that human behaviours are functions of the person and their environment. When these were applied to a group, there was the hypothesis that the participants would perform positively and for the collective good, if the conditions were right. Relationships were seen within their surrounding field and the group as an entity in itself.

Encounter groups then developed as a gradual integration of several theories and techniques, but the goal remained the same: it was all about the experience (the here-and-now) that could bring change. The general values of interpersonal congruence, exploration, intense emotional expression, self-disclosure, and confrontation were at the core of the three branches:

Carl Rogers's *basic encounter* finds the group sitting in a circle and interacting, relating verbally with emphasis on the congruence of each communication. The facilitator participates equally, and their role is to embody the congruence, empathy, and unconditional positive regard that can encourage change through relationships. Each participant's contribution is valued equally, affirming in this way the individual personal power as well as the importance of the egalitarian nature of peer-to-peer interaction (versus the quality of the therapist–client relationship). This branch of encounter has influenced the contemporary 'process groups' in psychotherapy trainings.

Will Schutz's *open encounter* was an attempt to bring the whole mind–body continuum in the encounter. Here the group sits in a circle, but there is a more fluid structure (e.g. sitting on cushions rather than chairs and removing the furniture) as the group uses movement and action for expression and interaction. Experimentation is encouraged by the facilitator who is responsible for checking where the energy of the group goes. They, therefore, have the role of suggesting movements, group exercises, and anything that would allow the energy in the group to flow.

The *Synanon encounter*, developed by Chuck Dederich, was a more specialised branch as it was initiated in groups for substance abusers who lived in residential settings. Here the approach is intensive; the group turns to one participant, makes them their target of attack, and cross-examines them about their attitudes and behaviours. This kind of confrontational approach was believed to help a substance abuser to break through their addictive patterning and defences but has been proved rather harmful, and often abusive, so it has not survived in our times.

With the pandemic of COVID-19 there has been an interesting flourishing of online international encounter groups that shift the image of people sitting in or moving within a circle, to a series of boxes on a screen that connect people from different continents and diverse backgrounds. We could see this movement as the renaissance of encounter groups, influenced by globalisation and online technologies.

CO-COUNSELLING

Co-counselling was founded by Harvey Jackins in the early '50s (later renamed as 'Re-evaluation counselling communities'), and it has since developed in some different reworkings of its original form, including the most prominent one, 'Co-counselling international' co-founded by John Heron and Tom and Dency Sargent in 1974.

This is an approach that epitomises the egalitarian principle of humanistic psychology as it is based on the idea that personal change happens through reciprocal peer counselling.

Co-counsellors take in turns the roles of the client and therapist, they have equal time, and they interact from a place of equality. Everyone engaged in this movement must go through the fundamentals of the school within which they practise and from there they create co-counselling pairs, which sometimes can last a lifetime.

Unlike any other therapy session, it is the person who is in the role of the client who is in charge of their session, and the person who is the counsellor does their best to listen and give their full attention. The aim of this co-constructed process is for the counsellor to support the client to work through whatever material they bring in the session, in a mainly self-directed way.

Safety and confidentiality are of paramount importance as is the boundary of roles beyond the co-counselling process.

The various schools differ in their view of interventions by the counsellor, but the values of non-directivity and encouragement are shared as the approach has been created for people with no specialised training but with a desire and commitment to change and socio-political awareness.

RECOMMENDED READING

Brown, L. (2018). *Feminist therapy* (2nd ed.). Washington, DC: American Psychological Association.

Brownell, R. (Ed.). (2008). *Handbook for theory, research, and practice in Gestalt therapy*. Newcastle: Cambridge Scholars.

Friedman, H., & Hartelius, G. (Eds.). (2015). *The Wiley-Blackwell handbook of transpersonal psychology*. Oxford: Wiley-Blackwell.

Kauffman, K., & New, C. (2004). *Co-counselling: The theory and practice of re-evaluation counselling*. London: Routledge.

Lago, C., & Charura, D. (Eds.). (2016). *The person-centred counselling and psychotherapy handbook: Origins, developments and current applications*. Berkshire: Open University Press.

Schneider, K., Bugental, J., & Fraser Pierson, J. (Eds.). (2001). *The handbook of humanistic psychology*. Thousand Oaks, CA: Sage.

Stewart, I., & Joines, V. (2012). *TA today: A new introduction to transactional analysis* (2nd ed.). Wycomb: Lifespace Publishing.

van Deurzen, E., Craig, E., Längle, A., Schneider, K.J., Tantam, D., & du Plock, S. (Eds.). (2019). *The Wiley world handbook of existential therapy*. Chichester: John Wiley & Sons Ltd.

Yalom, I. (1970). *The theory and practice of group psychotherapy*. New York: Basic Books.

REFERENCES

Cain, D., Keenan, K., & Rubin, S. (Eds.). (2016). *Humanistic psychotherapies: Handbook of research and practice*. Washington, DC: American Psychological Association.

Cooper, M., O'Hara, M., Schmid, P., & Bohart, A. (Eds.). (2013). *The handbook of person-centred psychotherapy and counselling* (2nd ed.). Hampshire: Palgrave Macmillan.

Cortright, B. (1997). *Psychotherapy and spirit: Theory and practice in transpersonal psychotherapy*. Albany, NY: State University of New York Press.

Clarkson, P. (1992). *Transactional analysis psychotherapy*. London: Routledge.

Erskine, R. (1997). *Theories and methods on an integrative transactional analysis*. San Francisco, CA: TA Press.

Hargaden, H., & Sills, C. (2002). *Transactional analysis: A relational perspective*. London: Routledge.

Hill, M. (Ed.). (2011). *Feminist therapy as a political act*. New York: Routledge.

Johnson, M. (2007). *The meaning of the body: Aesthetics of human understanding*. Chicago, IL: University of Chicago Press.

Polster, E., & Polster, M. (1973). *Gestalt therapy integrated: Contours of theory & practice*. New York: Vintage Books.

Pitts, C., & Kawahara, D. (Eds.) (2020). *Radical visionaries: Feminist therapy pioneers, 1970–1975*. London: Routledge.

Robertson, C., & van Gogh, S. (Eds.). (2018). *Transformations in troubled times: Re-Vision's soulful approach to therapeutic work*. Forres: TransPersonal Press.

Rogers, C. (1970). *On encounter groups*. New York: Harper Collins.

Sanders, P. (Ed.). (2012). *The tribes of the person-centred nation* (2nd ed.). Ross-on-Wye: PCCS Books.

Schneider, K. (Ed.). (2007). *Existential-integrative psychotherapy: Guideposts to the core of practice.* London: Routledge.

Wilber, K. (2000). *Integral psychology: Consciousness, spirit, psychology, therapy.* Boston, MA: Shambhala Publications, Inc.

Woldt, A., & Toman, S. (Eds.). (2005). *Gestalt therapy history, theory, and practice.* Thousand Oaks, CA: Sage.

Yalom, I. (1980). *Existential psychotherapy.* New York: Basic Books.

5

BEYOND SCHOOLISM AND TOWARDS BRIDGES
POST-'70S APPROACHES IN PSYCHOTHERAPY

Pure form therapies (e.g. psychoanalysis, cognitive therapy, person-centered or existential therapy) can be placed at the beginning of the timeline of therapies. From the '70s, though, the field moved towards a more integrative direction, with an emphasis on what equips the therapist best, what works for clients, and how theories (Western and Eastern) can be bridged in a way that makes sense in an ever-changing world. Neuroscience has also contributed to the changing scene of therapy, and although it's beyond the scope of this book to describe all the different neuro-influenced therapy approaches, I want to acknowledge them as forms of integrative therapies (e.g. neuro-linguistic psychotherapy which is a systemic imaginative method of psychotherapy with an integrative–cognitive approach). Next are some of the many new approaches that have been developed with these ideas in mind.

INTEGRATIVE PSYCHOTHERAPIES: INTEGRATION, ECLECTICISM, OR PLURALISM?

The integrative therapy approach crystalised into a strong and coherent force in the late '70s. It later redeveloped into eclectic therapies and has produced the pluralistic model more recently. Today, integrative psychotherapy is the most popular descriptive term for this

DOI: 10.4324/9780367824334-6

kind of therapies, and there are more than 450 different approaches that belong to this umbrella term.

We can trace back the search for integration from the '30s and all the way up to the '70s when there was a more conscious effort to respond to the so-called shortcomings of the three main schools/traditions on psychotherapy (i.e. psychoanalysis, behaviourism, and humanism) and a movement that saw psychotherapy 'after schoolism'. It was also the therapists' needs for more effective ways of helping clients that drove this movement for integration and maybe, also, the need for dialogue and bridge building between orientations.

There are three different approaches to integration:

(1) *Theoretical integration*: here the integration happens on the level of concepts and methods, and it is an attempt to create a meta-theoretical model of integration that helps make sense of the seeming contradictions between theories.
(2) *Assimilative integration*: this is the process of gradual assimilation of techniques and concepts from several approaches into a therapist's original orientation. The internal consistency of the emerging model is achieved by the therapist's experience. The latter allows them to incorporate empirically supported interventions and theoretical concepts that are compatible between them and with the therapist's original training, and at the same time they support the therapist to respond to their client's needs in a more attuned and flexible way.
(3) *Common factors approach*: here integration happens according to the areas of commonality amongst approaches (e.g. the idea that therapy can be helpful or the belief that change can happen).

Eclecticism was developed as a response to the need for an immediate flexibility from the therapist's side for what seems best for the client and their particular problem at each moment. It is an approach based on empirical research and focuses on interventions. Arnold Lazarus developed this further into technical eclecticism which bases the choice of intervention on the clients' needs and research evidence.

The *pluralistic model*, in Mick Cooper and John McLeod's view, is a form of integrative psychotherapy. However, these proponents postulate that it differs from other integrative approaches in being both a perspective and a practice, and because it puts emphasis on the levels of roles (i.e. client–therapist dialogue) and orientations. It is an approach that the two theorists developed to reconceptualise the clients' needs and desires as a priority and then, consequently, have the therapist adjust their theoretical stance and practice according to these needs and desires. This position stems from Emmanuel Levinas's idea that everyone is an 'Other' to everyone else and therefore unique; thus, in therapy, all clients bring their unique needs. This is achieved by emphasising – and encouraging – the meta-communication between client and therapist in relation to goals, tasks, and methods of therapy. Cooper and McLeod advocate that a therapist can adopt elements and techniques from several approaches if this is for the best of the client. In their view the therapist seems to have a continuously fluid ontological stance, and their main lens of looking at therapeutic relationships is what suits their clients. We could say that in the pluralistic model integration is seen as something theoretical and practical that happens in each session, rather than a long-term and conscious process that takes place within the therapist.

Here are a couple of other examples of integrative or eclectic therapy models:

- Emotion-focused therapy (EFT – or process-experiential therapy), first conceived by Laura Rice and Leslie Greenberg and further developed in more recent years by Robert Elliott. This is an approach that integrates active methods from Gestalt and the wider humanistic therapies, as well as from neuroscience, dialectical constructivism, and attachment theory. It is a protocol-based and task-focused process-guiding approach.
- Somatic experiencing (SE) is an alternative form of therapy developed by Peter Levine. It focuses on the bottom-up processing of trauma-related responses via internal sensations. Its roots can be traced back to Reich's body psychotherapy and more directly to Elsa Gindler's and Charlotte Selver's *sensory awareness*; it is the foundation for several body-oriented psychotherapies in the US and internationally. SE has also been influenced by Stephen Porges's neuropsychological theory on the polyvagal system and the wider practice of shamanism.

MINDFULNESS-ORIENTED PSYCHOTHERAPY: A MERGING OF BUDDHIST AND WESTERN PSYCHOLOGY

Mindfulness is the English translation for the Pali word 'sati' that is used in Buddhist psychology to denote awareness, attention, and the process of remembering. As a process, and not a state, we can understand mindfulness as a way of learning to experience life as a unified whole, a way of relating to all experience – whether that is positive, negative, or indifferent – and a way of reducing the impact of life's difficulties.

With the dawn of spiritually inclined approaches to psychotherapy in the '60s and '70s, there was an inevitable turn towards Buddhist psychology and philosophy. The therapeutic relationship was then seen under the prism of therapist and client paying attention to the phenomena in the shared space and time, increasing awareness of thoughts, feelings, and actions and cultivating an embodied presence for both parts. Other earlier attempts for bridging the two philosophical worlds of East and West can be traced in Jung's, Fromm's, and Horney's works from the late '30s and through the '40s and '60s.

From the therapist's perspective, this umbrella of approaches encourages attention with empathy, true presence, and deep listening. We can identify the humanistic psychology foundations in the qualities expected by a therapist: acceptance and non-fixing attitude, non-judgemental listening, trust, openness to what the client brings each time, letting go, the cultivation of the felt sense, and mutuality of experiences with the client.

Mindfulness–informed psychotherapy is also recognised as a third wave CBT approach and can be divided into two categories:

(1) Mindfulness-based psychotherapy: this is an integrative model of mindfulness and cognitive behavioural approaches in which clients are taught certain mindfulness skills to regulate their attention and feelings. Some of the approaches in this category are as follows:
   • Dialectical behaviour therapy (DBT): see Chapter 3 for more information.
   • Acceptance and commitment therapy (ACT): same.
   • Mindfulness-based cognitive therapy (MBCT): a set of mindfulness skills and techniques applied to cognitive therapy

and with clients diagnosed with depression. It teaches clients to observe their thoughts.

- Mindfulness-based stress reduction (MBSR): a time limited (8–10 weeks) mindfulness training, usually within a group-based format, for the support of clients with both physical and mental health problems.

(2) Mindfulness-informed psychotherapy: this category encompasses a more subjective use of mindfulness and Buddhist concepts by the therapist. It is the therapist who brings mindfulness in the therapy room, but they do not explicitly teach their clients any mindfulness practices or skills. Rather, the therapist, by embodying the qualities of mindful presence, creates a therapeutic environment that promotes these qualities within the therapeutic relationship.

Considering all the separate theories we have explored so far, what feels helpful or unhelpful when thinking about integrating theories in therapy?

How are true presence, deep listening, and awareness embodied and demonstrated in your everyday life, and do you have someone in mind who has acted as a role model for you?

FAMILY THERAPIES: SYSTEMS AND INDIVIDUALS

The aftermath of the Second World War was evident in the sharp increase of the demand for mental health services. Inevitably, the problems the world was facing had an impact on families. So, the '50s found a few pioneering psychiatrists (e.g. Murray Bowen, Carl Whitaker, Nathan Ackerman, and Gregory Bateson) developing therapy approaches for individual clients that included family members too.

The '60s and early '70s was the period when specific schools of family therapy became established (see the works of Salvador Minuchin, Jay Haley, Virginia Satir, and James Framo), and the '70s brought family therapy outside the consulting room and into mental health services, something that exists even to this day.

Family therapy – also known as systemic therapy – deals with the problems an individual or a system present within the relational context of their lives and social networks with significant others. It aims to change the interactions between family members as a way to improve both intra-psychic and interpersonal functioning. Couple therapy is also included in the umbrella of family therapies. It focuses on the couple subsystem of a family unit or any romantic relationship.

The wider 'context' (i.e. community, society, and culture) and systemic assumptions are at the core of the more contemporary family therapy approaches, thus the shift to the term 'systemic therapy' as it better represents the attention that is now paid to the impact of wider systems and social contexts on clients' psychological development and emotional well-being.

There are two kinds of family therapy definition:

(1) Head count definition: the understanding here is that family therapy is defined by the number of family members attending therapy simultaneously. It's a form of conjoint therapy definition.

(2) Systems-focused definition: here the distinction is on the focus of therapy rather than who attends the sessions. If the explicit focus is on improving family interactions, then it does not matter whether only one member of the family attends therapy.

Before we explore the different family therapies, it will be helpful to understand the importance of 'systems theory'. According to this theory the whole is greater than the sum of its parts. It is a theoretical framework that helps to understand the interactions between and among different parts of the family/system, as well as the implications of the produced dynamics on the nature of the system.

Some foundational and contemporary models of family therapy are described as follows:

• *Structural*: founded by Minuchin, this is a model interested in the family structure and its dimensions of boundaries, alliances, and distribution of power. Its scope is to alter the structure and the consequent interactions in order to achieve the desired change.

• *Strategic*: here the origins of a problem in the system are not important; thus, its brief nature is aimed at altering problematic and long-term communication patterns, as well as generating different ways of interactions that go beyond the usual problems. This model included the Mental Research Institute (MRI), the Palo Alto model, Haley's work, and the Milan group that introduced the one-way mirror and a whole family therapists' team.

- *Experiential*: this is a model that emphasises the here-and-now experience of the client(s) in the therapy room, as well as authentic emotional experiences and the lifting of defences. The technique of 'family' sculpture is one widely used, where a specific family member is asked to symbolise their perception of the family dynamics by physically arranging the rest of the family in the therapy room. Family constellations is also a contemporary approach that grew out of the original systemic approaches, but it highlights the experiential element.
- *Psychoanalytic*: here transgenerational patterns are looked at via 'genograms' (family maps), and the process focuses on bridging togetherness and individuality. Bowen, the founder of this approach, tried to bring together traditional individual psychoanalysis with family therapy theories.
- *Cognitive-behavioural*: the interventions target those cognitions that result in problematic behaviours.
- *Postmodern*: this cluster of approaches bring together the influence of context, clients' subjectivities, and the social construction of individual realities. Narrative therapy by Michael White and David Epston and solution-focused family therapy by Steve de Shazer and Insoo Kim Berg belong to this cluster.
- *Integrative*: this is a wider cluster of therapies that includes those models that are influenced by more than one theory (e.g. multidimensional family therapy, family constellations, functional family therapy, or psychoeducational family therapy).

RECOMMENDED READING

Evans, K., & Gilbert, M. (2005). *An introduction to integrative psychotherapy.* Hampshire: Palgrave MacMillan.

Germer, C., Siegel, R., & Fulton, P. (2016). *Mindfulness and psychotherapy* (2nd ed.). New York: The Guildford Press.

Nichols, M., & Davis, S. (2019). *The essentials of family therapy* (7th ed.). Hoboken, NJ: Pearson Education.

REFERENCES

Finlay, L. (2015). *Relational integrative psychotherapy: Engaging process and theory in practice*. Oxford: Wiley, Blackwell.

Lebow, J. (2014). *Couple and family therapy: An integrative map of the territory*. Washington, DC: American Psychological Association.

Woods, S. (2019). *Mindfulness-based cognitive therapy: Embodied presence and inquiry in practice*. Oakland, CA: Context Press, New Harbinger Publications.

6

EMBODIED AND CREATIVE APPROACHES
BRINGING THE MIND–BODY CONTINUUM AND CREATIVITY BACK TO OUR ATTENTION

BODY PSYCHOTHERAPY AND BODY-ORIENTED PSYCHOTHERAPY

It is hard to define the beginning of the history of body psychotherapy, but in its more theorised form it owes its existence to Wilhelm Reich. In its current form it encompasses a very wide range of practices, thus the extension of the name to body-oriented psychotherapy too. For the purposes of this book, I will concentrate on the most distinctive theories and approaches, and I signpost the reader to the recommended reading for a more expansive database of the existing approaches.

Pierre Janet was the first psychologist to introduce the idea of the body holding information and being a main access point to feelings. He looked at movement and its intentionality as well as the causality between muscular contraction and neurotic structures as early as 1885.

Ferenczi and Adler, as we saw in Chapter 2, also showed interest in the impact of embodied processes in the development of personality and in accessing unconscious material and trauma through their patients' bodies.

It was not until 1933, though, when Reich published his work *Character Analysis* that we can see the first foundations of body psychotherapy. In that seminal work, Reich deviated from his original

DOI: 10.4324/9780367824334-7

psychoanalytic talking approach and put the foundations for what would be later called body psychotherapy. His work even influenced Anna Freud on her theory of the ego and the mechanisms of defence.

REICH'S THEORY OF PERSONALITY DEVELOPMENT AND OF THERAPY: A RADICAL REVIEW OF THE FOCUS IN PSYCHOANALYSIS

Reich was one of the most promising protégés of Freud, but his radical ideas and his intention to bring together psychoanalysis and Marxism resulted in his expulsion from all psychoanalytic circles in the '30s. His was a one-body psychology that did not put emphasis on intra-psychic phenomena and object relations. According to Reich, our early childhood experiences shape both our personality and our body. He saw internalisation as an embodied process. This is demonstrated in body tensions as a result of negative experiences and repressive forces. He named this process *sculpting* of a *character*. The next step is the development of a *character armour*, which is a complex of muscle and tissue tensions. This *armouring* is our survival strategy in childhood as in this way we can contain our repressed feelings and our embodied tensions – a type of psychic economy called *frozen history*. The build-up of various armourings form our basic *character* type, depending on the time and way a trauma occurred, as well as on its resolution. Adulthood finds us clinging to this neurotic holding pattern, out of fear or a need of safety; thus, ignoring our innate desire for freedom.

Another important aspect of personality development is the circulation and expression of energy through our body. We can imagine a healthy energetic cycle that moves from tension to charge to discharge and finally to relaxation. Any energy that exists in a repressed situation or conflict needs to be expressed as a feeling so that our experiences can be fully integrated. For Reich sexual energy is primary, and its blocking in the body is seen as the source of neurosis, character traits, and social ills.

Therapy takes the form of *character analysis*, rather than symptomatology analysis. A systematic interpretation and confrontation of the client's defensive functions brings release and freedom. Reich's approach was precise and powerful and characterised by confrontation. He used direct body work techniques whilst working on breathing patterns, to bring traumas into the consciousness with the aim of resolution. Successful therapy meant that the client's natural libidinal energy was restored, and therefore, they regained their capacity for joy in their life and work.

The second generation of body psychotherapists, the Neo-Reichians, are Reich's direct students and clients, who took his theory and developed it further or integrated it with other theories. They founded the main post-war body psychotherapy trainings in the 1970s and focused on energy as the connecting force for the mind–body, feelings, and spirit. *Life-force* and *vitality* were the main concepts used for understanding neuroses. The most prominent figure in that generation was Alexander Lowen who, initially with John Pierrakos, developed *bioenergetics*. Lowen drew a systematic mapping of particular neurotic complexes situated in particular body parts and encouraged their vocal expression. He also re-emphasised the importance of verbal interpretation and worked with his clients whilst standing up (vs. lying down on the couch) to facilitate a more open breathing pattern and to introduce *grounding* as an embodied technique. Lowen's approach was based on Reich's plea for *liberating the energy* and aimed at emotional discharge.

Pierrakos's approach extended from bioenergetics into a more psycho-spiritual level and aimed at facilitating the liberation of the core self; thus, its name, *core energetic therapy*. Reich's daughter, Eva, developed her own approach, *gentle bioenergetics*. Eva Reich's work was mainly with babies born at home or premature and kept in incubators. She introduced the very light touch of *butterfly massage* as a preventative method for early energetic contraction (see the minimal or absent tactile contact for this client group) setting in and becoming chronic.

The later Neo-Reichians formed the third generation of body psychotherapists, and they took a more phenomenological turn, combining the philosophy with the character-analytical tradition and aiming at exploring beyond the clients' consciousness. The schools of this generation teach mindfulness, respect for the clients' defences, as well as recognition and resolution of the latter, and they have integrated, refined, and crossed between modalities. Some of the most influential figures and their approaches are as follows:

- Gerda Boyesen and *biodynamic psychotherapy*: Boyesen enriched the thinking of the use of touch in psychotherapy and introduced the relational kind of massage, biodynamic massage. The aim is to reach the client's unconscious as they are simultaneously expected to be active in the process by verbalising arising images or sensations. The use of touch is at the boundary of self and other and involves the nervous system.
- Ron Kurtz and *hakomi*: Kurtz combined several embodied practices and created his own approach that helps clients access who they could or should be. Kurtz was more interested in the emotional construct behind body and tension patterns, rather than in their interpretations.
- David Boadella and *biosynthesis*: this is an approach that emphasises the integration of physical, emotional, and mental life processes and is process-oriented. With specific techniques, the therapist follows and develops the client's internal signals and movement manifestations. Silvia Specht Boadella contributed to the development of David Boadella's theory by adding transpersonal aspects.
- Stanley Keleman and the *somatic process work*: Keleman's approach focuses on the blocks and armouring of energetic flow both on the muscles as well as on the soft tissues of the body. It aims to remove those blocks to deepen one's connection to themselves, the world, and the other than human.
- Charles Kelley and *Radix work*: Radix is the life force, the primary cause underlying all of life, and Kelley's work is a refinement of bodily tensions, through physical techniques, to reach one's potential. He saw his approach more as a form of education rather than of psychotherapy.
- Jack Lee Rosenberg and *integrative body psychotherapy (IBP)*: as a multi-theory and practice (Gestalt and transpersonal psychotherapy, object relations, self psychology, yoga, bioenergetics, breathwork), IBP aims to integrate somatic and conscious awareness. The work is on physical, energetic, emotional, and spiritual levels and facilitates the exploration of one's inner core of wisdom and reaching a fulfilling grounded sense of self.

The fourth generation of body psychotherapists coincides with the relational turn in psychotherapy and trainings that brought the therapeutic relationship and the intersubjective field at the forefront. Bernd Eiden and Jochen Lude, founders of the well-known Chiron training in London, opened the path for several generations of relational body psychotherapists by initiating the shaping of an approach with humanistic orientation, but also informed by psychodynamic theories. This is a holistic and integrative approach that places the relationship, the therapist's use of their own body, re-enactments, spirituality, and the functional unity of body and movement in the centre of processing.

In the theories and practice of this generation, there is a deepening of the understanding of transferential and countertransferential material and processes, and there is curiosity on the relationship within one's body, with other people's bodies, and with the in-between bodies.

In the UK there has been a collective project that promotes a contemporary view of the theory and practice of body psychotherapy by creating bridges with other contemporary theories and research (e.g. relational psychoanalysis, neuroscience). Nick Totton's work (*embodied-relational therapy*) has highlighted the importance of embodiment as a process that directly implies relationship; Roz Carroll's integration of relational psychoanalysis and dance movement psychotherapy has placed the moving body–mind at the forefront of embodied intersubjectivity; Michael Soth's *fractal self* extended practice beyond the notion of wholeness; Asaf Rolef Ben-Shahar (*integrative mindbody therapy*) brings body, mind, and soul in one and interrelated entity. Bill Cornell, in the USA, has drawn a picture of therapy of two different body–minds engaging in a project of mutual interest with the understanding that both therapist and client will affect and be affected by the process.

To summarise this vast and diverse approach, I will try to bring together some shared points across all generations and approaches that might help you, the reader, to visualise the focus and some of the practices.

Some basic principles

In body psychotherapy one's body is seen as a source of information about their state of being, the well of their feelings and memories, a more accessible entry point for psychological change, and the actual vehicle for the building of the therapeutic relationship and for interventions. One's body is as significant as, and no different from, their mind. Here we also need to consider the quality of the relationship to one's own body as a formative aspect of how they experience the world and nature, and of their attitude towards their sexuality and gender. Body psychotherapy uses a developmental and characterological framework to understand the structure of one's body, as well as its activity. Therefore, embodied interventions aim to facilitate a new experience for the client and their sensations, expression, and movement.

Observations of body posture, movement, breathing pattern, and muscle tension are used to capture the client's characteristic attitude and to identify blocked or interrupted energy. The therapeutic process and relationship encourage the liberation of these blocks and models ways of self-regulation. Embodied self-awareness gives more access to the client's body inherent life energy and, through therapy, they can dissolve those patterns that cause *muscular armouring*, in Reich's words.

Techniques

Body psychotherapy uses embodied techniques in the process of implementing the previously mentioned principles. The first generations were more directive than the fourth generation who see the therapeutic relationship from a two-way perspective, thus not engaging in the dynamic of the therapist 'doing' things to the client.

Here are some widely used techniques that are used even beyond body psychotherapy that some of you might be familiar with, given their popularity in today's well-being-focused world:

- Anchoring in the body
- Grounding
- Focusing on breathing
- Containment and attention to the 'centre' of one's body
- Methods of touch
- Mindfulness
- Movement techniques
- Body awareness

Have you ever noticed where your body gets blocked when you hold some difficult feelings?

What image do you have of your body and the tensions it holds on behalf of the whole mind–body continuum?

Of the previously mentioned techniques, which one(s) do you practise/are you familiar with/have you heard of?

Finally, I would like to pay tribute to what we can broadly call *body therapies* (e.g. body–mind centering (BMC), somatic therapy) as these are approaches that stemmed from body psychotherapy and used embodied and somatic practices but which do not use the therapeutic relationships, transference dynamics, unconscious material, or defences in a systematic and focused way. There the focus is on the client's body and the release of developmental stuckness, unpleasant feelings, or movement re-education, and re-patterning.

THE ARTS THERAPIES

With this term I mean the umbrella of psychotherapeutic approaches that use the arts (i.e. art, music, drama, and dance) as their main means of emotional expression and processing.

All arts therapies derive from one or more of the theoretical schools mentioned earlier in the book and therefore tend to have a shade of theoretical affiliation, which changes according to each continent-country and professional training. In the same note some of the approaches have two or more terms, for example dance movement psychotherapy and dance/movement therapy. This is because of professional affiliation differences across the several countries where the approaches are practised, taught, and regulated. There is, though, some sort of consensus about what each approach and practice involve.

The arts therapies are therapies in their own right and should not be confused with artistic and therapeutic practices applied in settings like hospitals for rehabilitation and community inclusion. Equally, the arts therapies have led their own professional way, separate from the generic use of artistic processes within talking therapies. It is also interesting to see the emergence of more eclectic forms, such as the *integrative arts therapies*, as an equivalent to the integrative tendency in talking therapies. *Expressive (arts) therapies* are also an eclectic model that offers clients a range of expressive modalities. All arts therapies are practised either individually or in groups and can support people of all ages, abilities, backgrounds, and at all stages of life.

The arts have been used as healing and medicinal means at various times and in various cultures across history. The examples of ancient rituals that involved music or drama or dance and the therapeutic symbolism of art making in ancient artifacts highlight the importance of arts in humans' well-being. The arts therapies take this step further by utilising each art form to facilitate expression, communication, and processing towards catharsis and healing. Depending on the client group the arts therapies can use the option of verbal communication; but there is the overall understanding that because arts participation and response don't depend on any speaking ability or skill, the arts therapies are particularly effective for people who have difficulty communicating verbally or when trauma creates the sense that words are not enough.

ART THERAPY (AT) OR ART PSYCHOTHERAPY

AT is a therapy approach that uses tactile and visual media (i.e. drawing, painting, collage, clay, printmaking, photography, puppets, masks, etc.) for the facilitation of the clients' self-expression, self-awareness, and growth, and as a means of communication between therapist and client. It is based on the ideas of the healing value of image-making, of the life-enhancing power of the creative process, and of the necessity of non-verbal communication of thoughts and feelings. Here the artistic expression is a visual communication of the unbearable. It's not only a different language but also a tool for the exploration of feelings, the reduction of stress, or the resolution of problems. Jung saw art creations not as sublimation or displacement but as integrators.

In AT the client is an interpreter of their own work, and the therapeutic potential is seen both in the making and the viewing of the art. The therapeutic process is illuminated by the artistic symbolism and metaphors used and is facilitated within the continuum of creator(client)–artefact–therapist. An art therapist can also make art alongside of or in response to their clients, depending on the first's theoretical approach and training. The fundamentals of *symbolising* and *seeing* explore what happens when people create (*symbolising*) and perceive (*seeing*) art.

Historically we can trace the first practices of AT in as early as the '30s when artists provided art sessions for patients with mental health problems in various settings. Since then, though, AT has expanded its clinical focus and has become a primary form of treatment for a wider range of clients. Adrian Hill coined the term AT when he described his experience of art work in the hospital where he was treated for tuberculosis. However, Margaret Naumburg is seen as the 'mother' of AT with her *dynamically oriented art therapy* approach in psychiatric settings, influenced by Freud and Jung and emphasising art as *symbolic speech*. Naumburg expanded AT beyond the constraints of an 'activity based' treatment and with a non-directive principle in mind. She also positioned AT closer to the interpersonalists in psychoanalysis; therefore, for her, two elements were vital: (1) the active interpersonal relationship between therapist and client, and (2) the clients' free associations on their creations rather than any pure interpretation of them by the therapist. One of Naumburg's contemporaries, Edith Kramer, shifted the emphasis from therapy onto art and developed her *art as therapy* approach in educational settings, focusing on the healing power of the creative process and on the Freudian defence mechanism of sublimation as a central parameter in the therapeutic experience. During that first wave of art therapists ('40s–'70s) Hanna Kwiatkowska contributed with her research and the development of family AT, and Elinor Ulman with her publications.

From the '70s on, a broader range of applications and theoretical perspectives are introduced in AT and social action becomes the focus when *community arts studios* started offering opportunities for creating, something like Adler's *social clubs*.

Today, AT has a broader and more eclectic orientation, including psychodynamic, humanistic, systemic, and learning and developmental theories.

DANCE MOVEMENT PSYCHOTHERAPY (DMP) OR DANCE/MOVEMENT THERAPY

DMP is a multisensory approach that both nurtures individuality and enhances the understanding of the self in relation to the other(s) through the therapeutic relationship. It enables emotional expression with the use of movement and dance, which are then consequently processed in non-verbal (see movement, movement analysis, and drawing) and verbal ways. The use of props (e.g. stretch clothes, scarves, balls) facilitates the non-verbal connection of therapist and client, as well as the externalisation of intra-psychic processes.

DMP as a therapy discipline was first established in the USA in the 1940s. Marian Chace was influenced by Sullivan's interpersonal psychiatry when she started her work with war veterans in hospitals. Mary Whitehouse based her approach, *authentic movement*, on Jung's theories and specifically on the concept of *active imagination*. They were the pioneers that then encouraged several more of their contemporaries to form their own approach of dance therapy – as the approach was initially called – based on both a movement technique (e.g. Mary Wigman's German dance improvisation or Bird Larson's natural dance) and one of the fundamental theories of personality and development.

From that initial wave the following practitioners-theorists emerged:

* Blanche Evan with Adlerian influences
* Liljan Espenak with Freudian and Adlerian influences
* Trudi Schoop with her rather transpersonal approach (she did not write a clear statement on her theoretical influences)
* Alma Hawkins with her humanistic growth model

A second wave of pioneers developed in the UK in the 1970s, spearheading the more structured clinical practice and trainings that made DMP a separate discipline from dance practice or therapeutic dance.

Further to the clinical practice during the first years of the development of DMP, an important question came up: what is the method of observation and evaluation of the health-dysfunction continuum? The answer to this question came from Rudolf Laban's work on movement analysis (*Laban Movement Analysis* – *LMA*) and later from Warren Lamb (movement observation and analysis for corporate environments – *Body Code*), Irmgard Bartenieff (*Bartenieff Fundamentals*), Marion North (*Personality Assessment through Movement*), Judith Kestenberg (*Kestenberg Movement Profile* – *KMP*), and Martha Davies (*Movement Psychodiagnostic Inventory* – *MPI*).

In DMP therapist and client are involved in a movement dialogue, and in the more relational branches of DMP, motion is seen as both an initiation and a response to what is brought into the intersubjective space by the client, as experienced via the therapist's subjectivity. *Mirroring, attunement*, and *synchrony* navigate the mutually initiated movement and dance. DMP is practised both with individuals and with groups, across all age groups and abilities and can be shaped in a structured (see different phases such as warm-up and process time) or free-flowing way, according to the therapist's own approach as well as the needs of each client group.

DRAMATHERAPY OR DRAMA THERAPY

Dramatherapy has been described as a therapy approach that systematically uses action methods (e.g. role-playing, story-making) and play for the facilitation of the clients' imagination, creativity, insight, and growth. The drama part is seen as containing the therapy, and the approach is both verbal and non-verbal, in the sense that it does not rely on spoken language only but puts great importance on embodiment and movement.

Dramatherapy is influenced by several psychotherapeutic theories and, thus, contains different paradigms. Its origins are in theatre and improvisation (see the schools of Constantin Stanislavski, Bertolt Brecht, Antonin Artaud, Peter Brook, and Jerzy Grotowski), dating all the way back from ancient Greece and the cathartic aspect of theatre and drama. There are no specific individuals that shaped the formation of the approach, but there is the view that Vladimir Iljine's *therapeutic theatre*, Nikolai Evreinov's *theatrotherapy*, and Jacob Moreno's *psychodrama* opened the path for the generation after them to envision a separate therapy approach.

There are some basic processes that contain the dramatherapeutic process, and these have the client at their centre:

- *Dramatic projection:* this is the client's emotional and intellectual involvement with their material with the use of dramatic forms, such as characters and puppets
- *Playing:* clients can experiment within the *play space* offered in dramatherapy, without feeling that there will be consequences and therefore can explore their material alongside their therapist
- *Transformation:* through the dramatic processes and the therapeutic relationship, clients can explore and express their material and

then their experience of the problems that brought to therapy is transformed

In dramatherapy therapist and client(s) use roles and characters to explore life experiences; props to facilitate their expression; their bodies to explore their self, image, and/or relationships; movement to experiment with new ways of relating; scripts, stories, and myths to act out themes; and dramatic rituals to process life experiences. The dramatherapeutic space is perceived as a 'concrete' place that inspires safety to develop one's dramatic reality; the latter allows for dramatic distancing, which consequently engages the therapeutic dyad/group both with the inner world and its imagination, as well as with the outer space of the therapy room.

Dramatherapy is mostly facilitated in a structured form with a warm-up, focusing around the subject of the work time, the main activity with the involvement through the expressive forms, the closure with all the *de-roling* from characters/roles/improvisation required, and the completion as the final part of the session for integration of all material explored.

MUSIC THERAPY (MT)

MT is based on the premise that music experience is therapeutically transformative and complete in and of itself. Positive changes in emotional well-being and communication are facilitated through the engagement in live musical interaction between client and therapist. This interaction can take the forms of improvising, re-creating/performing, composing, and/or listening. Music and songs are created through the use of voice, musical instruments, and body sounds, whilst music imaging involves listening to music, or feeling its vibrations in the case of clients with hearing impairments – and responding with free associations, images, body sensations, feelings, and memories.

An MT session is facilitated in an interpersonal setting where the client improvises alone, with the therapist, or in a group, and their improvisation can represent something non-musical – for example feelings or a story – (*referential improvisation*), or it can be organised around a certain musical consideration with the meaning stemming purely from relationships within the music itself (*non-referential improvisation*). The live music interactions between therapist and client establish the therapeutic relationship, and the music therapist is an active participant in the process. Music is seen as a symbolic language, and it function as a therapeutic medium; it is a representation and expression of one's inner world, and as such it raises spiritual awareness.

MT can have two levels of engagement: (1) when music is used as psychotherapy and the therapeutic issue is accessed and processed through creating and listening to music solely – that is the use of words is not needed, and (2) when the therapy is music-centered and the therapeutic issue is accessed and processed through creating and listening to music, but verbal guidance and interpretation accompany the music experience wherever it is relevant to the client and the therapeutic process.

In the USA in the early 20th century, there were courses in *musicotherapy*, and these are seen as the predecessors of today's MT. Thayer Gaston and William Sears are seen as the US pioneers in MT whilst the more professional direction of MT started in the '50s with Juliette Alvin developing her own eclectic model of free improvisation (*the Alvin model*) and establishing one of the very first trainings in the UK at the Guildhall. At the same time Paul Nordoff and Clive Robbins developed *the Nordoff–Robbins model* which relied on Rudolf Steiner's anthroposophy, humanistic psychology, as well as existential psychotherapy and transactional analysis elements. This model and subsequent training are creative and improvisational.

Other distinguished models are as follows:

- Helen Bonny's *guided imagery music* (*GIM*) with a Jungian and transpersonal psychology influence. Here the client enters an altered state of consciousness whilst they also dialogue with the therapist, and they get involved in imaging to specially designed music programmes.
- Mary Priestley's analytically oriented MT.
- Rolando Benenzon's MT model (mainly in South America).
- Isabelle Frohne-Hagemann's and Fritz Hegi's Gestalt and musical psychodrama model.

- Behavioural MT where the music is the main factor in the overcoming of problems – not the therapeutic relationship – and it is used as a stimulant, relaxant, or reward. Clifford Madsen is one of the main developers of this approach.

PSYCHODRAMA PSYCHOTHERAPY (PP)

As the first recognised form of group psychotherapy, PP dates back to the beginning of the 20th century when Jacob Moreno embarked on his lifelong journey of creating a therapy that would have spontaneity and creativity at its core. It is a structured and action-based psychotherapeutic approach, inspired by improvisation theatre and where group and individual action are perceived as ways of looking at one's life as it moves, whilst experiencing what happened and didn't happen in the described situation.

In PP all scenes take place in the present, whether the theme for exploration is from the past or a future aim. Each member of the group is a therapeutic agent aiming to offer an experience of being understood and emotionally and physically held, whilst maintaining the distance of not being enmeshed in the original story. A member of the group becomes the *protagonist* who brings the theme they want to explore and acts it out. The therapist takes the role of the *director* who is responsible for both guiding the session and monitoring the progress of the process. The *auxiliary egos* are qualified assistants who act as co-therapists, playing complementary roles in the protagonist's story, as well as directing the latter and taking observers' stance of the scenes that are played out. The other members of the group can act both as *audience* and as actors enacting either the theme of the session or parts of life, as these are seen through the protagonist's eyes. A specific space, the *stage*, is used to enable the protagonist to represent their inner world and create possibilities.

The action during the dramatisation is equally important to what the clients, in all the different roles, say. The aim is for them all to gain greater insight into their and others' situations so that they achieve a sense of mastery of their thoughts and feelings and their strengths and resilience are increased.

Sessions are structured with a warm-up, the action (*enactment*), and the final sharing. Some of the major techniques used in PP are *double* (the auxiliary ego stands behind/beside the protagonist and adopts the latter's mind–body expressions whilst enhancing their expression with what they feel is implicit in the protagonist's enactment), *role reversal* (the protagonist swaps roles with the group member/director with whom they interact and places themselves in the psychological shoes of that person), and *sociometry* (each member places a hand on the shoulder of the person they select according to the question/criteria presented by the director – everyone clarifies their choice afterwards and deals with potential confrontations). Psychodrama is now used beyond the therapy field and in education, trainings, conflict transformation, and community building. One of its offshoots is *sociodrama* that is conducted on the level of macro-sociology, addressing social issues and inter-group conflict in an experiential way and with the aim of transformation, equality, and tolerance in society.

> Do you consider creativity as part of your way of living, exploring the world, and/or expressing yourself?
>
> How have the arts influenced your life and emotional and relational expression?

'COUSIN' APPROACHES

I have chosen to include play therapy and ecotherapy in this chapter. I see them as part of the wider family of embodied and creative therapies that have challenged the dominance of the talking therapies and have brought an alternative perspective to the question of what is helpful for a client in distress, what is effective, where change stems from, and what is the individual's connection with their self, body, whole way of being, and nature.

PLAY THERAPY (PT)

PT stems from the efforts of the early pioneers of therapy to apply their theories and practices with adults to children who were acknowledged as separate from their caregivers, as individuals with emotional needs. Play was seen as a non-intrusive and natural way of establishing rapport, facilitating communication, encouraging emotional expression, and potentially providing some healing.

The first mention of the term PT was made by the psychoanalyst Hermine Hug-Hellmuth in 1921, who published a paper on separate methods of analysing child-patients as opposed to adult ones. As we saw in Chapter 2, Melanie Klein and Anna Freud established the two child psychoanalytic schools that influence child psychoanalysis even today. Around the same time Margaret Lowenfeld, a paediatric medicine professional in London, developed her own approach of child therapy and especially the use of sandtray and the creation of 'worlds' in sandtrays with small objects (the *world technique*). On the other side of the world, in the US, and in the '30s, David Levy was developing his *release therapy* for children who had experienced a stressful event or trauma; he would encourage the replay of the event and its reconstruction. Later, Gove Hambidge developed this approach further and renamed it as *structured PT*. Jacob Conn, at the same time, developed his *play interview* technique, where children were supported in expressing themselves through the use of family dolls. Joseph Solomon took this further and developed the approach of *active PT*. Here the therapist takes an active role in using dolls and other props to re-enact the child's problems.

The 'mother', though, of PT as we know it today is thought to be Virginia Axline, who developed the non-directive approach, influenced by Carl Rogers, called child-centered PT. Axline described some basic principles for her approach that have become the basis for most of the PT schools that developed from the '50s on. Warmth, permissiveness, accepting the child where they are, non-judgemental attitude, setting limits, and maintaining a belief in the child and their capacity for their own problem solving are some of them. Clark Moustakas took the child-centered element a step further by moving out of his chair and following his child-client to the space as the latter would use it. This is where the healing started to be focused on the therapeutic relationship.

Today PT encompasses a wide range of schools but equally has shifted away from model-specific treatments to more integrative approaches. The emphasis of the practice is on the functions of play as an emotional stabiliser and connector with significant others throughout the life span. It is defined as the systematic use of certain theoretical models in which the therapist uses and facilitates the therapeutic powers of play for the processing, prevention, and resolution of psychosocial difficulties for their clients, and for the achievement of their potential and optimal growth.

The therapeutic powers of play range from the facilitation of communication, self-expression, and access to the unconscious to the enhancement of social relationships, self-regulation, and increase of personal strengths. Some of the contemporary PT schools are as follows:

- *Theraplay®* by Ann Jernberg and Phyllis Booth: this is an approach that addresses ruptures or disruptions in the child–parent bonding experience by using nurturing touch, playful interactions, and focused eye contact. It is based on Bowlby's and Winnicott's theories.
- *Filial therapy* by Louise and Bernard Guerney: here parents and caregivers are involved in the therapy process as that is seen as an intergenerational process that needs to address issues on a societal level, seeing the lives of children being impacted by factors and events beyond the therapy room.
- *Developmental PT* by Viola Brody: with influences from DMP and Buber's 'I–Thou' concept, developmental PT starts the therapy process from where the child is developmentally and then supports them to move to the next developmental stages through the healing use of touch.
- *Experiential PT* by Carol and Byron Norton: play is seen here as the metaphor that carries the child's expression and feelings as they process experientially the information from their environment.
- *Ecosystemic PT* by Kevin O'Connor: an integrative approach to PT that brings together psychoanalytic, developmental, CBT, child-centered, and Theraplay® theories and practices.

There are also PT schools based on specific psychodynamic theories (e.g. Jungian and Adlerian Play Therapy), cognitive-behavioural theories, Gestalt theory (e.g. Violet Oaklander's well-known approach), etc.

ECOTHERAPY

Ecotherapy emerged as an approach out of the need for an alternative mode of therapy that addresses the issue of modern office-based mental health approaches and ways of living and being.

There are several terms used for nature-based therapies and, of course, all of them represent a certain or a cluster of schools: outdoor therapies, ecohealth, deep ecology, bush adventure therapy, and ecotherapy. I will use the latter term as it's the clinical practice of ecopsychology, and it is the most used term in the relevant literature and research.

It is important to understand what ecopsychology is before we explore its clinical practice. Ecopsychology studies the synergy between human emotional and overall well-being and the health and ecological integrity of the natural environment. It is a discipline that focuses on the enhancement of people–environment interactions and well-being. Ecotherapy encompasses all nature-based and environmentally sensitive therapeutic practices that address the focus of ecopsychology and aim to transform humans' relationships with nature.

All the previously mentioned approaches under the ecotherapy umbrella have some shared principles as new paradigms of health and well-being:

- Nature is incorporated as a partner in the therapy practice
- They pay respect and attention to physical and natural environments as these have a corresponding effect on humans
- Attention and intention are paid on the reciprocal influences between environmental forces and human actions
- They recognise the importance of the natural world in conceptualising mental health and understand wellness in connection to nature; thus, nature is seen as an active means of healing
- Eco-centric methods are used to restore the human connection with earth-based values
- Climate crisis and the human responsibility are addressed as part of the therapy process and clients are invited to take an active stance in their relationship to nature

Nature's restorative capacity is the main method of ecotherapy, and there is an increasing number of research to prove the psychological and physiological benefits of time spent in natural outdoor spaces (e.g. improved mood, reduced stress responses, and improved body attitudes). The term 'outdoor' involves a range of natural settings – from urban parks to remote wilderness. It also entails a spectrum of involvement in the actual therapeutic practice: it can be a passive backdrop to sessions that provides emotional regulation, or it can be fully incorporated through active techniques and the subsequent behavioural analysis – something like a third person in a one-to-one therapy or an extra layer of group dynamic in group therapy.

In practice ecotherapy is place-based and involves an active bodily engagement in the nature–human spectrum, whilst holding on to principles of ecological care. Nature is seen and encouraged to be experienced as place, metaphor, co-therapist, and a bodily felt aspect of one's therapy. The intensity of physical actions and interactions and interdependence with nature can vary from low (e.g. walking) to moderate (e.g. gardening) to high (e.g. living outdoors for days and engaging intermittently to group and/or individual therapy).

Since the use of time and space, as well as the focus of interactions and quality of relationships are different from the mainstream idea of therapy in offices, both therapist and client find themselves equal in the therapy experience but try at the same time to establish and maintain the needed reflective space for therapy to happen. Here both the wilderness and the therapeutic relationship are agents of change.

Ecotherapy can also be seen as part of the process of decolonising therapy in the sense that it embraces the long lost – or, better, force-fully erased – earth-based rituals and practices of indigenous people and addresses the effects of colonial practices of enforced silencing of cultures and their traditions.

Some more specific approaches that are now well-established in the West are equine and animal-assisted therapies, environmental expressive therapies, eco-arts therapies, wilderness therapy, garden and horticultural therapies, forest therapy, and surf therapy.

> How much play exists in your everyday reality and expression, and have you ever experienced play as an emotional stabiliser in your adult life?
> What is your emotional connection to nature?
> Are you aware of any emotional shifts when you are distressed or overwhelmed and choose to be outdoors versus indoors?

RECOMMENDED READING

Baim, C., Burmeister, J., & Maciel, M. (Eds.). (2007). *Psychodrama: Advances in theory and practice*. London: Routledge.

Buzzell, L., & Chalquist, C. (Eds.). (2009). *Ecotherapy: Healing with nature in mind*. San Francisco, CA: Sierra Club Books.

Case, C., Dalley, T., & Reddick, D. (2023). *The handbook of art therapy* (4th ed.). London: Routledge.

Jenning, S., & Holmwood, C. (Eds.). (2016). *Routledge international handbook of dramatherapy*. London: Routledge.

Jacobsen, S., Pedersen, I., & Ole Bonde, L. (Eds.). (2019). *A comprehensive guide to music therapy: Theory, clinical practice, research and training* (2nd ed.). London: Jessica Kingsley Publishers.

O'Connor, K., Schaefer, C., & Braverman, L. (Eds.). (2016). *Handbook of play therapy* (2nd ed.). Hoboken, NJ: John Wiley & Sons, Inc.

Payne, H. (Ed.). (2017). *Essentials of dance movement psychotherapy: International perspectives on theory, research and practice*. London: Routledge.

Staunton, T. (2002). *Body psychotherapy*. London: Routledge.

REFERENCES

Blanter, A. (2000). *Foundations of psychodrama: History, drama, and practice* (4th ed.). New York: Springer Link Publishing Company.

Bunt, L., & Stige, B. (2014). *Music therapy: An art beyond words* (2nd ed.). London: Routledge.

Chaiklin, S., & Wengrower, H. (Eds.). (2016). *The art and science of dance/movement therapy: Life is dance* (2nd ed.). New York: Routledge.

Harper, N., & Dobud, W. (Eds.). (2021). *Outdoor therapies: An introduction to practices, possibilities, and critical perspectives*. London: Routledge.

Hartley, L. (Ed.). (2009). *Contemporary body psychotherapy: The Chiron approach*. London: Routledge.

Jennings, S., Cattanach, A., Mitchell, S., Chesner, A., & Meldrum, B. (1994). *The handbook of dramatherapy*. London: Routledge.

Jones, P. (1996). *Drama as therapy: Theory, practice and research* (2nd ed.). London: Routledge.

Kottman, T. (2011). *Play therapy: Basics and beyond* (2nd ed.). Alexandria, VA: American Counselling Association.

Levy, F. (2005). *Dance movement therapy: A healing art*. Reston, VA: American Alliance for Health, Physical Education, Recreation & Dance.

Malchiodi, C. (Ed.). (2012). *Handbook of art therapy* (2nd ed.). New York: The Guilford Press.

Schaefer, C. (Ed.). (2011). *Foundations of play therapy* (2nd ed.). Hoboken, NJ: John Wiley & Sons, Inc.

Totton, N. (2003). *Body psychotherapy: An introduction*. Maidenhead: Open University Press.

EPILOGUE

By now you will have read either the entire book or parts of it and you will have either created a picture of the dominant Western therapy approaches, or you will have got a taste of the many and diverse traditional and indigenous healing approaches.

This epilogue feels like a good place for me to introduce you to a more critical and challenging view of therapy, one that takes responsibility for the creation and practice of approaches that have caused suffering, one that questions and acts upon the profession's and academic discipline's inequalities. Examples include conversion therapy (i.e. therapy that focuses on changing clients' sexual orientation, gender expression, or gender identification), trainings with a mainly white perspective on suffering and healing, and barriers for clients with physical and learning difficulties on accessing therapy and therapy spaces. When we consider such inequalities in therapy, we can begin to understand why the established normative therapy theories have given meaning to individual processes according to the gender-binary heterosexual, white privileged, abled body–mind regime.

Therapy has traditionally been an ethnocentric discipline, with a majority apolitical perspective, and it developed during Europe's colonial expansion period. Therefore, it has been influenced by – and mainly performs – the heterocolonial abled patriarchy that has

DOI: 10.4324/9780367824334-8

dominated our capitalist world and for the most part imposes and maintains invisibility for certain groups of people that don't fit into the accepted 'norm'. The different Western theories I have described in this book compete on their ideologies and conceptualisation of the problem of what it means to be human, leaving unexplored issues of modern power taxonomies (i.e. gender, race, class, abilities, etc.) and perpetuating the neoliberal forms of normativity that highlight inequalities in our world.

This is an invitation to consider therapy beyond society's fears of depatriarchalising, decolonising, and deheterosexualising our world, the psychic apparatus, and our mind–bodies. It is also a reminder to look at the bigger picture and consider personal problems as the result of social problems too. Intersectional differences highlight the complexities of identity, as well as of opportunities in life. Therefore, we need to consider how therapy needs to theorise and create practices beyond the usual European mode, to keep striving to become aware of constructs – for example race and gender – that create and recreate the binary or powerful and powerless, and to look carefully into its contribution to the historical trauma of systemic oppression of certain groups in our world. Maybe it's time therapy becomes in-submissive to powers that control the non-privileged, the marginalised, and therefore disrupt the cycle of oppression and discrimination. For this to happen we need to reconsider what is perceived as normal and to focus our theorising, researching, and practising – continuous processes – not just on improving access to therapy and information but also how therapy theory is metabolised and transferred in a complete and inclusive way.

Finally, it is now time for therapy to take a more rigorous political stance regarding the destruction of the earth's biosphere, that human-authored apocalypse that is leading the world to the Anthropocene extinction.

I hope this book has given you some thought to join the movement towards a therapy that needs to transition, a therapy free of the previously mentioned modern power taxonomies, no matter what your role in therapy is – client, therapist, trainee, trainer, curious fellow traveller. And as Foluke Taylor (2023: 20) says, 'Where and how else might we travel?'

RECOMMENDED READING

Preciado, P. B. (2022). *Can the monster speak?* London: Fitzcarraldo Editions.

Taylor, F. (2023). *Unruly therapeutic: Black feminist writings and practices in living room*. New York: W. W. Norton.

REFERENCES

Cameron, R. (2020). *Working with difference and diversity in counselling and psychotherapy*. London: Sage.

Czyzselska, J. C. (Ed.). (2022). *Queering psychotherapy*. London: Karnac.

hooks, b. (2000). *Feminism is for everybody*. London: Pluto Press.

lykou, s. (2021). Sociopolitical perspectives on trauma in a world in crisis: The personal is political revisited. In A. Chesner & s. lykou (Eds.), *Trauma in the creative and embodied therapies: When words are not enough* (pp. 7–18). London: Routledge.

Taylor, K.-Y. (Ed.). (2017). *How we get free: Black feminism and the Combahee River Collective*. Chicago, IL: Haymarket Books.

Turner, D. (2021). *Intersections of privilege and otherness in counselling and psychotherapy: Mockingbird*. London: Routledge.

Wark, M. (2023). *Love and money, sex and death*. London: Verso.

BIBLIOGRAPHY

Achan, G., Eni, R., Kinew, K., Phillips-Beck, W., Lavoie, J., & Katz, A. (2021). The two great healing traditions: Issues, opportunities, and recommendations for an integrated first nations healthcare system in Canada. *Health Systems and Reform*, 7(1), e1943814. https://doi.org/10.1080/23288604.2021.1943814

Asamoah, G., Khakpour, M., Carr, T., & Groot, G. (2023). Exploring indigenous traditional healing programs in Canada, Australia, and New Zealand: A scoping review. *Explore*, 19(1), 14–25. https://doi.org/10.1016/j.explore.2022.06.004

Atwood, G., & Stolorow, R. (1979/1993). *Faces in a cloud: Intersubjectivity in personality theory*. Northvale, NJ: Jason Aronson Inc.

Bagge, N., & Berliner, P. (2021). Psychotherapy and indigenous people in the Kingdom of Denmark. *Psychotherapy and Politics International*, 19(2), e1586. https://doi.org/10.1002/ppi.1586

Baim, C., Burmeister, J., & Maciel, M. (Eds.). (2007). *Psychodrama: Advances in theory and practice*. London: Routledge.

Barsness, R. (Ed.). (2018). *Core competencies of relational psychoanalysis*. London: Routledge.

Bateman, A., & Holmes, J. (2022). *Introduction to psychoanalysis: Contemporary theory and practice* (2nd ed.). London: Routledge.

Beck, J. S. (2021). *Cognitive behavior therapy: Basics and beyond* (3rd ed.). New York: The Guilford Press.

Blanter, A. (2000). *Foundations of psychodrama: History, drama, and practice* (4th ed.). New York: Springer Link Publishing Company.

Bodibe, R. C. (1992). Traditional healing: An indigenous approach to mental health problems. In J. Uys (Ed.), *Psychological counselling in the South African context* (pp. 149–165). Cape Town, South Africa: Maskew Miller Longman.

Brown, L. (2018). *Feminist therapy* (2nd ed.). Washington, DC: American Psychological Association.

Brownell, R. (Ed.). (2008). *Handbook for theory, research, and practice in Gestalt therapy*. Newcastle: Cambridge Scholars.

Bunt, L., & Stige, B. (2014). *Music therapy: An art beyond words* (2nd ed.). London: Routledge.

Buzzell, L., & Chalquist, C. (Eds.). (2009). *Ecotherapy: Healing with nature in mind*. San Francisco, CA: Sierra Club Books.

Cain, D., Keenan, K., & Rubin, S. (Eds.). (2016). *Humanistic psychotherapies: Handbook of research and practice*. Washington, DC: American Psychological Association.

Cameron, R. (2020). *Working with difference and diversity in counselling and psychotherapy*. London: Sage.

Case, C., Dalley, T., & Reddick, D. (2023). *The handbook of art therapy* (4th ed.). London: Routledge.

Chaiklin, S., & Wengrower, H. (Eds.). (2016). *The art and science of dance/movement therapy: Life is dance* (2nd ed.). New York: Routledge.

Clarkson, P. (1992). *Transactional analysis psychotherapy*. London: Routledge.

Cooper, M., O'Hara, M., Schmid, P., & Bohart, A. (Eds.). (2013). *The handbook of person-centred psychotherapy and counselling* (2nd ed.). Hampshire: Palgrave Macmillan.

Cortright, B. (1997). *Psychotherapy and spirit: Theory and practice in transpersonal psychotherapy*. Albany, NY: State University of New York Press.

Crozier, S., & Pizzini, N. (2019). Engaging with indigenous knowledge to shape a bicultural counselling programme in Aotearoa New Zealand. *Psychotherapy and Politics International, 18*(2), 1–21. https://doi.org/10.1002/ppi.1515

Czyzselska, J. C. (Ed.). (2022). *Queering psychotherapy*. London: Karnac.

Dryden, W., & Reeves, A. (2012). *The handbook of individual therapy* (6th ed.). London: Sage.

Durie, M. (1998). *Whaiora: Māori health and development* (2nd ed.). Melbourne, Australia: Oxford University Press.

Erskine, R. (1997). *Theories and methods on an integrative transactional analysis*. San Francisco, CA: TA Press.

Evans, K., & Gilbert, M. (2005). *An introduction to integrative psychotherapy*. Hampshire: Palgrave MacMillan.

Ewen, R. B. (2010). *An introduction to theories of personality* (7th ed.). New York: Psychology Press.

Ferguson, A., & Gutiérrez-Peláez, M. (2022). *Sándor Ferenczi: A contemporary introduction*. London: Routledge.

Finlay, L. (2015). *Relational integrative psychotherapy: Engaging process and theory in practice*. Oxford: Wiley, Blackwell.

Freedheim, D. (2002). *History of psychotherapy: A century of change*. Washington, DC: American Psychological Association.

Friedman, H., & Hartelius, G. (Eds.). (2015). *The Wiley-Blackwell handbook of transpersonal psychology*. Oxford: Wiley-Blackwell.

Fromm, E. (1942/1997). *The fear of freedom*. London: Routledge.

Germer, C., Siegel, R., & Fulton, P. (2016). *Mindfulness and psychotherapy* (2nd ed.). New York: The Guildford Press.

Gomez, L. (1997). *An introduction to object relations*. London: Free Association Books.

Gureje, O., Nortje, G., Makanjuola, V., Oladeji, B., Seedat, S., & Jenkins, R. (2015). The role of global traditional and complementary systems of medicine in the treatment of mental health disorders. *Lancet Psychiatry, 2*(2), 168–177. https://doi.org/10.1016/S2215-0366(15)00013-9

Hall, A., Poutu, M., & Wilson, C. (2012). Waka Oranga: The development of an indigenous professional organisation within a psychotherapeutic discourse in Aotearoa New Zealand. *Psychotherapy and Politics International, 10*(1), 7–16. https://doi.org/10.1002/ppi.1255

Haque, I., Chowdhury, A., Shahjahan, M., & Harun, G. (2018). Traditional healing practices in rural Bangladesh: A qualitative investigation. *BMC Complementary and Alternative Medicine, 18*, 62. https://doi.org/10.1186/s12906-018-2129-5

Hargaden, H., & Sills, C. (2002). *Transactional analysis: A relational perspective*. London: Routledge.

Harper, N., & Dobud, W. (Eds.). (2021). *Outdoor therapies: An introduction to practices, possibilities, and critical perspectives*. London: Routledge.

Hartley, L. (Ed.). (2009). *Contemporary body psychotherapy: The Chiron approach*. London: Routledge.

Haugh, S., & Paul, S. (Eds.). (2008). *The therapeutic relationship: Perspectives and themes*. Ross-on-Wye: PCCS Books.

Hill, M. (Ed.). (2011). *Feminist therapy as a political act*. New York: Routledge.

hooks, b. (2000). *Feminism is for everybody*. London: Pluto Press.

Incayawar, M., Wintrob, R., Bouchard, L., & Bartocci, G. (Eds.). (2009). *Psychiatrists and traditional healers: Unwitting partners in global mental health*. Chichester: Wiley-Blackwell.

Jacobsen, S., Pedersen, I., & Ole Bonde, L. (Eds.). (2019). *A comprehensive guide to music therapy: Theory, clinical practice, research and training* (2nd ed.). London: Jessica Kingsley Publishers.

Jenning, S., & Holmwood, C. (Eds.). (2016). *Routledge international handbook of dramatherapy*. London: Routledge.

Jennings, S., Cattanach, A., Mitchell, S., Chesner, A., & Meldrum, B. (1994). *The handbook of dramatherapy*. London: Routledge.

Johnson, M. (2007). *The meaning of the body: Aesthetics of human understanding*. Chicago, IL: University of Chicago Press.

Jones, P. (1996). *Drama as therapy: Theory, practice and research* (2nd ed.). London: Routledge.

Kapur, R. (1979). The role of traditional healers in mental health care in rural India. *Social Sciences & Medicine, Part B: Medical Anthropology, 13*(1), 27–31. https://doi.org/10.1016/0160-7987(79)90015-2

Karpf, F. (1953). *The psychology and psychotherapy of Otto Rank.* New York: Philosophical Library.

Kauffman, K., & New, C. (2004). *Co-counselling: The theory and practice of re-evaluation counselling.* London: Routledge.

Kennerley, H., Kirk, J., & Westbrook, D. (2017). *An introduction to cognitive behaviour therapy: Skills and applications* (3rd ed.). London: Sage.

Koithan, M., & Farrell, C. (2010). Indigenous native American healing traditions. *The Journal for Nurse Practitioners, 6*(6), 477–478. https://doi.org/10.1016/j.nurpra.2010.03.016

Kottman, T. (2011). *Play therapy: Basics and beyond* (2nd ed.). Alexandria, VA: American Counselling Association.

Lago, C., & Charura, D. (Eds.). (2016). *The person-centred counselling and psychotherapy handbook: Origins, developments and current applications.* Berkshire: Open University Press.

Laplanche, J., & Pontalis, J. B. (1967/1988). *The language of psycho-analysis.* London: Karnac.

Lebow, J. (2014). *Couple and family therapy: An integrative map of the territory.* Washington, DC: American Psychological Association.

Levy, F. (2005). *Dance movement therapy: A healing art.* Reston, VA: American Alliance for Health, Physical Education, Recreation & Dance.

lykou, s. (2021). Sociopolitical perspectives on trauma in a world in crisis: The personal is political revisited. In A. Chesner & s. lykou (Eds.), *Trauma in the creative and embodied therapies: When words are not enough* (pp. 7–18). London: Routledge.

MacLeod, S. (2014). Immrama: Journeys in indigenous Celtic shamanic practice. *A Journal of Contemporary Shamanism, 7*(1), 28–34.

Mahood, K. (2018). The man in the log: Tjukurpa wati minyma kutjaratjara. *The Monthly (Australia), 8.*

Malchiodi, C. (Ed.). (2012). *Handbook of art therapy* (2nd ed.). New York: The Guilford Press.

Mathibela, M., Egan, B., Du Plessis, H., & Potgieter, M. (2015). Socio-cultural profile of Bapedi traditional healers as indigenous knowledge custodians and conservation partners in the Blouberg area, Limpopo Province, South Africa. *Journal of Ethnobiology and Ethnomedicine, 11*, 49. https://doi.org/10.1186/s13002-015-0025-3

McKendrick, J., Brooks, R., Hudson, J., Thorpe, M., & Bennett, P. (2013). *Aboriginal and Torres Strait Islander healing programs: A literature review.* Canberra, Australia: The Healing Foundation.

Midgley, N. (2013). *Reading Anna Freud*. London: Routledge.

Mitchell, S., & Black, M. (2016). *Freud and beyond: A history of modern psychoanalytic thought* (2nd ed.). New York: Basic Books.

Montenegro, R., & Stephens, C. (2006). Indigenous health in Latin America and the Caribbean. *Lancet*, *367*, 1859–1869. https://doi.org/10.1016/S0140-6736(06)68808-9

Montiel Tafur, M., Crowe, T., & Torres, E. (2009). A review of curanderismo and healing practices among Mexicans and Mexican Americans. *Occupational Therapy International*, *16*(1), 82–88. https://doi.org/10.1002/oti.265

Moore, B., & Fine, B. (Eds.). (1990). *Psychoanalytic terms and concepts*. New Haven, CT: The American Psychoanalytic Association.

Naka, K., Toguchi, S., Takaishi, T., Ishizu, H., & Sasaki, Y. (1985). Yuta (Shaman) and community mental health on Okinawa. *International Journal of Social Psychiatry*, *31*(4), 267–274. https://doi.org/10.1177/002076408503100404

Ngaanyatjarra Pitjantjatjara Yankunytjatjara Women's Council Aboriginal Corporation. (2013). *Ngangkari: Traditional Aboriginal healers*. Alice Springs, Australia: Ngaanyatjarra Pitjantjatjara Yankunytjatjara Women's Council Aboriginal Corporation.

Ngoma, M. C., Prince, M., & Mann, A. (2003). Common mental disorders among those attending primary health clinics and traditional healers in urban Tanzania. *British Journal of Psychiatry*, *183*, 349–355. https://doi.org/10.1192/bjp.183.4.349

Nichols, M., & Davis, S. (2019). *The essentials of family therapy* (7th ed.). Hoboken, NJ: Pearson Education.

O'Connor, K., Schaefer, C., & Braverman, L. (Eds.). (2016). *Handbook of play therapy* (2nd ed.). Hoboken, NJ: John Wiley & Sons, Inc.

Payne, H. (Ed.). (2017). *Essentials of dance movement psychotherapy: International perspectives on theory, research and practice*. London: Routledge.

Peeters, L. (2010). The Marumali program: An aboriginal model of healing. In N. Purdie, P. Dudgeon & R. Walker (Eds.), *Working together: Aboriginal and Torres Strait Islander mental health and wellbeing principles and practice* (pp. 287–292). Canberra, Australia: Australian Government Department of Health and Ageing.

Pham, T., Richav, K., Wainberg, M., & Kohrt, B. (2021). Reassessing the mental health treatment gap: What happens if we include the impact of traditional healing on mental illness? *Community Mental Health Journal*, *57*(4), 777–791. https://doi.org/10.1007/s10597-020-00705-5

Pitts, C., & Kawahara, D. (Eds.) (2020). *Radical visionaries: Feminist therapy pioneers, 1970–1975*. London: Routledge.

Polster, E., & Polster, M. (1973). *Gestalt therapy integrated: Contours of theory & practice*. New York: Vintage Books.

Portman, T., & Garrett, M. (2006). Native American healing traditions. *International Journal of Disability, Development and Education*, *53*(4), 453–469. https://doi.org/10.1080/10349120601008647

Preciado, P. B. (2022). *Can the monster speak?* London: Fitzcarraldo Editions.

Quinn, S. (1987). *A mind of her own: The life of Karen Horney.* New York: Summit Books.

Rivera, E. (2005). Espiritismo: The flywheel of the Puerto Rican spiritual traditions. *Interamerican Journal of Psychology, 39*(2), 295–300.

Robertson, C., & van Gogh, S. (Eds.). (2018). *Transformations in troubled times: Re-Vision's soulful approach to therapeutic work.* Forres: TransPersonal Press.

Robertson, D. (2010). *The philosophy of cognitive-behavioural therapy (CBT): Stoic philosophy as rational and cognitive psychotherapy.* London: Karnac.

Rogers, C. (1970). *On encounter groups.* New York: Harper Collins.

Rustin, M., & Rustin, M. (2017). *Reading Klein.* London: Routledge.

Ryoko, S. (2014). *A society accepting of spirit possession: Mental health and shamanism in Okinawa.* London: Routledge.

San Roque, C. (2012). Aranke, or in the long line: Reflections on the 2011 Sigmund Freud award for psychotherapy and the lineage of traditional indigenous therapy in Australia. *Psychotherapy and Politics International, 10*(2), 93–104. https://doi.org/10.1002/ppi.1262

Sanders, P. (Ed.). (2012). *The tribes of the person-centred nation* (2nd ed.). Ross-on-Wye: PCCS Books.

Schaefer, C. (Ed.). (2011). *Foundations of play therapy* (2nd ed.). Hoboken, NJ: John Wiley & Sons, Inc.

Schneider, K. (Ed.). (2007). *Existential-integrative psychotherapy: Guideposts to the core of practice.* London: Routledge.

Schneider, K., Bugental, J., & Fraser Pierson, J. (Eds.). (2001). *The handbook of humanistic psychology.* Thousand Oaks, CA: Sage.

Schouler-Ocak, M., & Kastrup, M. (Eds.). (2020). *Intercultural psychotherapy for immigrants, refugees, asylum seekers and ethnic minority patients.* New York: SpringerLink.

Schwartz, J. (1999). *Cassandra's daughter: A history of psychoanalysis.* New York: Viking.

Shange, S., & Ross, E. (2022). "The question is not how but why things happen": South African traditional healers explanatory model of mental illness, its diagnosis and treatment. *Journal of Cross-Cultural Psychology, 53*(5). 503–521. https://doi.org/10.1177/00220221221077361

Shankar, B., Saravanan, B., & Jacob, K. (2006). Explanatory models of common mental disorders among traditional healers and their patients in rural South India. *International Journal of Social Psychiatry, 52*(3), 221–233. https://doi.org/10.1177/0020764006067215

Shimoji, A. (1992). Interface between shamanism and psychiatry in Miyako Islands, Okinawa, Japan: A viewpoint from medical and psychiatric anthropology. *The Japanese Journal of Psychiatry and Neurology, 45*(4), 767–774. https://doi.org/10.1111/j.1440-1819.1991.tb00515.x

Solera-Deuchar, L., Mussa, M., Ali, S., Haji, H., & McGovern, P. (2020). Establishing views of traditional healers and biomedical practitioners on collaboration in mental health care in Zanzibar: A qualitative pilot study. *International Journal of Mental Health Systems*, 14(1), 1–10. https://doi.org/10.1186/s13033-020-0336-1

Staunton, T. (2002). *Body psychotherapy*. London: Routledge.

Stewart, I., & Joines, V. (2012). *TA today: A new introduction to transactional analysis* (2nd ed.). Wycomb: Lifespace Publishing.

Stolorow, R. (2013). Intersubjective-systems theory: A phenomenological-contextualist psychoanalytic perspective. *Psychoanalytic Dialogues*, 23(4), 383–389. https://doi.org/10.1080/10481885.2013.810486

Taylor, F. (2023). *Unruly therapeutic: Black feminist writings and practices in living room*. New York: W. W. Norton.

Taylor, K.-Y. (Ed.). (2017). *How we get free: Black feminism and the Combahee River Collective*. Chicago, IL: Haymarket Books.

Totton, N. (2003). *Body psychotherapy: An introduction*. Maidenhead: Open University Press.

Trower, P., Jones, J., & Dryden, W. (2015). *Cognitive behavioural counselling in action* (3rd ed.). London: Sage.

Tudor, K. (Ed.). (2011). *The turning tide: Pluralism and partnership in psychotherapy in Aotearoa New Zealand*. Auckland, Aotearoa New Zealand: LC Publications.

Turner, D. (2021). *Intersections of privilege and otherness in counselling and psychotherapy: Mockingbird*. London: Routledge.

van Deurzen, E., Craig, E., Längle, A., Schneider, K.J., Tantam, D., & du Plock, S. (Eds.). (2019). *The Wiley world handbook of existential therapy*. Chichester: John Wiley & Sons Ltd.

Waldram, J. (Ed.). (2008). *Aboriginal healing in Canada: Studies in therapeutic meaning and practice*. Ottawa, Canada: Aboriginal Healing Foundation.

Walter, M., & Fridman, E. (Eds.). (2004). *Shamanism: An encyclopedia of world beliefs, practices and culture*. Santa Barbara, CA: ABC-CLIO.

Wark, M. (2023). *Love and money, sex and death*. London: Verso.

WHO. (2002). *WHO traditional medicine strategy 2002–2005*. World Health Organization.

WHO. (2013). *Mental health action plan 2013–2020*. World Health Organization.

Wilber, K. (2000). *Integral psychology: Consciousness, spirit, psychology, therapy*. Boston,8 MA: Shambhala Publications, Inc.

Woldt, A., & Toman, S. (Eds.). (2005). *Gestalt therapy history, theory, and practice*. Thousand Oaks, CA: Sage.

Wolff, R. (2014). The effects of integrative healthcare on Peruvian Indigenous groups. *Studies by Undergraduate Researchers at Guelph*, 7(2), 5–12.

Wood, H. (unknown date). Healing in the Celtic world. In S. Clancy & F. Nicholson (Eds.), *Land, sea and sky*. Online Book.

Woods, S. (2019). *Mindfulness-based cognitive therapy: Embodied presence and inquiry in practice*. Oakland, CA: Context Press, New Harbinger Publications.

Yalom, I. (1970). *The theory and practice of group psychotherapy*. New York: Basic Books.

Yalom, I. (1980). *Existential psychotherapy*. New York: Basic Books.

Yen, J., & Wilbraham, L. (2003). Discourses of culture and illness in South African mental health care and indigenous healing, Part I: Western psychiatric power. *Transcultural Psychiatry*, *40*(4), 542–561. https://doi.org/10.1177/1363461503404005

INDEX

Note: numbers in *italics* indicate a figure